Answers
to
Everything

Other Oliver-Nelson books by Todd Temple

How to Rearrange the World

How to Become a Teenage Millionaire

Creative Dating
(with Doug Fields)

52 Ways to Show Aging Parents You Care
(with Tracy Green)

52 Simple Ways to Teach Your Child About God

Answers
to
Everything*

*Actually, 259 answers to questions about life, death, love, sex, money, God, and the future

TODD TEMPLE

THOMAS NELSON PUBLISHERS
Nashville

To Darrell, Elaine, Missy, and Randy;
my partners and friends at 10 TO 20

Published in Nashville, Tennessee, by Oliver-Nelson Books, a division of Thomas Nelson, Inc., Publishers, and distributed in Canada by Lawson Falle, Ltd., Cambridge, Ontario.

Unless otherwise noted, the Bible version used in this publication is the HOLY BIBLE: NEW INTERNATIONAL VERSION. Copyright © 1973, 1978, 1984 by the International Bible Society. Used by permission of Zondervan Bible Publishers.

Printed in the United States of America.

Library of Congress Cataloging-in-Publication Data

Temple, Todd, 1958–
    Answers to everything : actually, 259 answers to questions about life, death, love, sex, money, God, and the future / Todd Temple.
       p.   cm.
    Includes bibliographical references (p.   ).
    Summary: Provides answers to a variety of questions, including "Is there a right way to kiss?" "What does it take to become a spy?" "How do you learn hang gliding?" and "How do you catch AIDS?"
    ISBN 0-8407-9568-8
    1. Life skills—Miscellanea—Juvenile literature. 2. Adolescence—Miscellanea—Juvenile literature.   [1. Life skills—Miscellanea.
2. Questions and answers.]   I. Title.
HQ2037.T46   1992
305.2'35—dc20   92-22917
                                                CIP
                                                 AC

1 2 3 4 5 6 — 97 96 95 94 93 92

CONTENTS

ACKNOWLEDGMENTS

Had this book been entitled *Answers to Something,* writing it would have been a solo act. But for answers to *everything,* I needed help. Here are the people I turned to, and for whose encouragement and assistance I am extremely grateful:

Doug Fields and *Tracy Green,* coauthors of some of my previous books, for letting me excerpt our work for this book;

Elaine Read, Cathy LeVeque, and *Shawn Barnett,* for their contributions on many subjects both serious and silly;

Lou Douros, for providing answers to several key questions, including the Goldilocks Dilemma and the ages-old Peter Piper Problem;

Patrice Johnell, for her wisdom in health and fitness—and the ability to convey it simply and clearly (and for being a pretty great sister);

Melissa Paton, for her reckless sense of adventure in agreeing to research the overwhelming variety of subjects covered in this book, and for editing, organizing, and encouraging at every step of the project.

A Confession

I confess. The title of this book is a bit of an exaggeration. This book doesn't contain the answers to *everything*. The periodic table of elements is missing, for one thing. Also absent is the recipe to my mom's lasagna. And as to the migratory patterns of the Patagonian pigeon...not a peep. Sorry.

But let's concentrate on what *is* in here. Basically, the book gives answers to four kinds of questions:

1. Questions you may be too embarrassed to ask...
   Is there a right way to kiss? (165)
   How can you tell if sex organs are "normal size"? (22)

2. Questions you wouldn't know *who* to ask...
   What does it take to become a spy? (128)
   What's it like to get a nose job? (6)

3. Questions you'd never think to ask...
   How do you learn hang gliding? (114)
   How do you write a love poem? (164)

4. Questions you already know the answer to, but hey, it wouldn't hurt to hear it again...
   What happens if you're stopped for driving under the influence? (146)
   How do you catch AIDS? (20)

Obviously, many questions in this book could take dozens of pages to answer, which would make a very thick book. But I figured you wouldn't read a book you couldn't lift, so I cut and slashed and scrunched each answer to make it short and sweet. If you're really interested in a topic, you can get more complete and detailed information on it in fatter books.

Last thing. I'm not an expert on all these subjects. But I *am* good at knowing where to look for the answers. I consult books and magazines and friends and experts to help me assemble the information in my writing. One of the key places I look for answers is the Bible. It doesn't answer every question (it's silent on the subject of snowboarding, for instance), but it covers the really important ones. And it gives me perspective for answering the rest. The Bible—and the God it talks about—influenced my writing. Which means some of these answers will be different from what you get from TV, textbook, or teacher. I hope you find the difference refreshing.

Okay, end of confession. Now it's time to start asking questions.

Todd Temple
Del Mar, California

Appearance

1. What's the first thing people notice when they meet someone?
2. You try to watch what you eat, but when you get around your friends, you break your diet. How can you stay on your diet without giving up your social life?
3. If food makes you fat, how come you don't lose much weight when you stop eating?
4. What's the simplest way to stay healthy and control weight?
5. How can you tell if you're exercising properly?
6. What's it like to get a nose job?
7. What other kinds of cosmetic surgery do people get?
8. Can certain kinds of clothing make you look thinner and taller?
9. What do you wear if you want to look shorter or broader?
10. Can steroids make a person bigger?
11. You have yellowish teeth. What can you do?
12. What causes acne?
13. How do you get rid of acne?
14. What is cellulite?
15. Is sunbathing dangerous?
16. What hairstyle is best for you?
17. How do you pick the right eyeglass frames?
18. Can a tattoo be removed?
19. Who decides what's going to be popular?

1. What's the first thing people notice when they meet someone?

Your clothes, your hair, your smile—these are all important to a first impression. But the very first thing people notice about you is your *posture:* how you sit, stand, and walk.

Let's say you're walking toward a guy at the far end of a hall. The light isn't very good, and besides, he's too vain to wear his glasses in public, so he can't see your face or your hair. He can't even see what you're wearing. All he sees is a moving silhouette. The *way* that silhouette moves becomes his first impression of you.

Okay, so you probably don't meet most people in such a setting (if you do, maybe you should find a new hangout). But regardless of the room, the first thing the eye picks up is movement. If you shuffle, stroll, or strut (or saunter, slide, or skate), you're making a statement about yourself.

The second thing the eye perceives is shape. This has more to do with the *alignment* of your body parts than their *size:* some short people stand tall; some thin people have a posture that looks, well, *fat.*

Conduct a visual survey. Go to a mall or busy street corner and observe how different people walk, sit, or stand. Check out the angle of the head, the position of the arms, how they lift their feet. Try to determine how happy or confident people are by their posture. Now experiment with your posture—what kind of message are you sending with your silhouette?

If you'd like to improve your posture, just do what Mom and Dad have been telling you: shoulders back, head level, back straight. If you feel like you're standing at attention, you probably look it—relax a little.

Posture is a self-perpetuating confidence builder. When you sit, stand, and walk with casual confidence—whether you *feel* confident or not—people treat you as a confident person. This makes you feel confident, which improves your posture, which...you get the picture.

◆

2. You try to watch what you eat, but when you get around your friends, you break your diet. How can you stay on your diet without giving up your social life?

Eating is a basic physical need, like sleeping or eliminating. Well, you conquered the nine o'clock bedtime and potty training. Why is taking control of this other physical need so difficult? The problem is that eating isn't just a physical thing. It's a social thing.

It's a rare day when you and your friends meet after school to take a nap. That's because sleeping really isn't a social thing, unless you count slumber parties. Eliminating hasn't been a social thing since that day in kindergarten when you wet your pants during show-and-tell.

But eating is a social experience. It's the one ingredient you find at every gathering—from the pizza at a late-night study session to the Thanksgiving turkey to the obligatory dinner on a dinner-and-a-movie date. Going on a food diet can feel like going into social seclusion.

How to Keep Your Diet *and* Your Friends   Changing your food habits doesn't have to wreck your social life. A bit of planning can make a big difference.

Spoil your meal. Do what your mom always told you not to do: snack before the meal. Fill up on fruits or vegetables before going out to eat. You'll eat less at your meal and won't get caught drooling over someone else's.

Take charge. Plan things to do that don't involve the consumption of vast quantities of food. You're probably not the only one dealing with a diet. The others will appreciate your efforts.

Team up. It's always easier to break a habit when you have a partner, especially when the habit is a social one. Pick the times when staying on your diet is the toughest (e.g., Friday nights), and plan low-temptation alternatives.

Talk about it. A good friend *wants* to help you and doesn't mind avoiding things that would cause you to stumble. And the time will come when he or she will need the same kind of consideration from you.

...and Your Family Family time is an endangered ritual in most homes. If meals are the only times you're together, a diet can mess things up. It doesn't have to.

Tell your folks. Parents worry about your health—it's in their job description. Explain your diet and how you're taking care of the essentials your body needs (if your diet is "stop eating," they won't be satisfied...and neither will you). Most parents would be happy to adjust the menu a bit.

Plan the meal. Prepare a meal that fits into your diet and still works for everyone else. If you're dieting right, this shouldn't be difficult.

◆

3. If food makes you fat, how come you don't lose much weight when you stop eating?

It seems logical: stop eating; lose weight. Here's what really happens. When you go without food for a while, your body starts conserving energy. Within twenty-four to forty-eight hours your metabolism slows 15 to 30 percent. In other words, your body is now burning fewer calories, making fat loss *more* difficult.

It gets worse. When you break your fast, your body takes its time getting back up to full fat-burning speed so it can't keep up with this new batch of fuel you're feeding it. The *next* time you diet, your metabolism drops faster; break it again and your metabolism increases even slower than the first time.

With each successive diet, the weight loss is slower and the regaining of weight is faster.

It's like driving in bumper-to-bumper freeway traffic. Every time you switch to the lane that's moving, it stops and another one starts to move. The people who were patient to creep along in their own lane got home twenty minutes ago.

It's the same way with the people who are successful at losing the weight and keeping it off. They avoid on-again, off-again games with their metabolism and stick to a simple combination of proper eating and exercise.

Smart Eating Tips

- Make the act of eating a ritual. Set the table and enjoy it!
- Confine your eating to one place in the house: no eating in front of the TV, on the couch, or in your room.
- Eat slowly.
- Use small dishes.
- Keep healthy alternatives on hand (e.g., carrot sticks instead of candy bars).

———————— ◆ ————————

4. What's the simplest way to stay healthy and control weight?

Eat smart and exercise right.

You don't have to be a biochemist to figure out the right foods to eat—your body shouts out the answers. Smart food makes you feel light and alert and satisfied. Greasy, fatty, or sugary food makes you feel heavy and a little sick in the stomach. If you're not in touch with your feelings, feel your face. Good foods make it kissable; bad foods make it look... well, like the food itself.

Once you've adjusted your eating to match the obvious, fine-tune it with help from the experts. Most of the major news magazines regularly run articles on nutrition, written in words we nonbiochemists can understand. You'll learn about the long-term effects of certain foods and vitamins—things that your body won't tell you until it's too late.

When most of us were kids, *exercise* wasn't even in our vocabulary. What grown-ups call exercise, kids call *life*: running, jumping, riding, swimming, skating, climbing, playing. Maybe it lost its allure when they started calling it physical education. But whatever you call it, it's not an option.

Any exercise will do you good, but low-intensity aerobic exercise is especially good at shifting your body into a fat-burning mode: brisk walking, bicycling, running, swimming. The fat-burning part kicks in about 20 minutes into the exercise. Until then, your body burns glycogen, a nonfatty fuel that's already stored in the muscles.

---- ◆ ----

5. How can you tell if you're exercising properly?

Aerobic exercise uses your lungs and heart as efficiently as possible, strengthening your cardiovascular system. Aerobic exercise needn't be superstrenuous. The important factors are how long and how often you exercise. You can tell if you're getting the maximum benefit from your exercise by doing a little bit of math:

Start with the number 220...
Subtract your age from it...
Multiply that first by 75 percent and then by 85 percent.

Your target heart rate should fall between the two numbers when you exercise—your heart rate being beats per minute. During exercise, find a pulse point on your wrist or neck (the neck is easier to find, but press only one side or you could pass out).

Count your heartbeats for 6 seconds…
Multiply by 10.

If your heart rate is slow, speed up. If it's fast, slow down.

———————— ◆ ————————

6. What's it like to get a nose job?

First of all, the surgery is called *rhinoplasty,* which is enough to stop most people right there. A cosmetic surgeon reshapes the nose by cutting the skin and cartilage and (are you sitting down?) by breaking and carving the bone. A nose job costs $2,000 to $5,000 and leaves your face black and blue for about two weeks.

Most teenagers who consider a nose job decide to wait until they're older. Here's why:

Faces Change   Your legs may have stopped growing, but your face hasn't. (You don't believe that? Look at your mom's senior picture.) Okay, so your nose probably won't shrink in the next few years, but there's little sense in reshaping it now to fit a face that's still changing.

Styles Change   It would be a shame to spend all that money for a small nose just before big noses (or bumpy or pudgy or pointy ones) become all the rage.

Priorities Change   Your appearance will still matter to you in a few years but never as much as it does right now. It's generally best to postpone such a big decision until the pressure lessens.

———————— ◆ ————————

7. What other kinds of cosmetic surgery do people get?

You name it, surgeons can do it. After nose jobs, here are the most popular kinds:

Breast Implants   About 20 percent of these operations are for women who've suffered from breast cancer. Most of the rest are enlargements. People's perceptions of the "ideal" size fluctuate from year to year. It seems odd that so many women would alter their bodies to pursue a fickle image.

In light of recent findings that indicate potential severe problems caused by breast implants, this procedure is currently receiving intense scrutiny by the medical profession.

Facial Surgery   Noses aren't the only things people play with. You can have your chin lengthened, your cheekbones raised, and your ears pinned back.

Ethnic Surgery   This is a scary one. Plastic surgeons report a rise in the number of black men and women who follow Michael Jackson's lead and have noses narrowed and lips thinned. Some Asians have had surgery to reshape the epicanthic fold in the eyelids to give the face a more Western look.

———————— ◆ ————————

8. Can certain kinds of clothing make you look thinner and taller?

Yes. If you want people to look at you up and down instead of side to side, wear clothes with thin vertical stripes and lines. Dark clothing, especially black and navy blue, tends to minimize your size. Tight-fitting clothing makes heavy people look heavier.

———————— ◆ ————————

9. What do you wear if you want to look shorter or broader?

Wear clothes with horizontal lines. Choose shirts with broad shoulders and wide sleeves. If you're thin, tight-fitting clothes will make that fact obvious.

◆

10. Can steroids make a person bigger?

Steroids are derivatives of the male hormone testosterone that alter the body's chemistry and add strength and muscle bulk. But they can also make your system go haywire. You can end up with high blood pressure, heart attack, impotency, and psychological problems such as aggressiveness, paranoia, and delusions.

The real kicker is, they can backfire. Instead of augmenting your growth, they can suspend it: you end up stronger but shorter, for example. Regardless of whether you buy them legally or illegally, steroids are simply not worth the risk. And if you do buy them on the street, you never know what you're really taking or where it came from.

◆

11. You have yellowish teeth. What can you do?

Teeth come in a range of colors, from pale yellow to grayish. If yours are naturally yellow (i.e., the color isn't from tartar or from playing with that yellow food coloring again), you can...

Bleach Them The dentist paints your teeth with oxidizing solution, then shines a special light on them to activate the process. The procedure is painless (if you don't count the anxiety of a dentist visit) and costs $750 to $2,000 or more, depending on the number of visits it takes. Some dentists can give you a home bleaching kit that's cheaper, but you can damage your gums if you don't do it right. By the way, don't use fabric bleach. It may work, but you'll be too dead to care.

Veneer Them   Bonding is the method of choice among actors and TV people. A thin plastic or porcelain veneer is bonded to the front of the tooth with adhesive resin. No drills are used. The procedure costs about $450 per tooth and lasts about five years.

Cap Them   Actors and TV news reporters did this before bonding became popular. The dentist grinds down your front teeth (the ones that show when you smile) and sticks shiny white caps over them. It involves a lot of drill time and costs $500 or more per tooth. The caps last about five years.

Leave Them Alone   By the time you get them snow white, the natural hues will be in vogue, and you'll be yearning for your old yellows. Wait a year. If you're still stuck on white by then, talk to your parents and your dentist.

———————— ◆ ————————

12. What causes acne?

Your skin comes direct from the factory with a moisturizing system already installed. The moisturizer is called sebum; it's manufactured and delivered by the sebaceous glands. When a gland gets blocked by dirt, the sebum can't get to the surface. With nowhere else to go, it oozes into deeper layers of skin. The deep skin layers don't like this and register their complaint by becoming inflamed. A zit is born.

Acne is so common during adolescence because of hormones your body produces that shift your sebaceous glands into overdrive (oh, the wild wonders of puberty!). These hormones also affect the emotions, which have their own effects on acne. It's a one-two punch.

———————— ◆ ————————

13. How do you get rid of acne?

A facial mole is fashionable. A sun-scorched nose is sporty. Dimples are divine. But acne... it's atrocious.

Until the day comes when zits are a fashion statement, here's what you can do about them:

- Wash your face with warm water and soap to clean out skin pores.
- Don't pick at your face (Mom's right on this one). This spreads infection and makes scarring more likely.
- Wash your hands frequently. Dirt and grease from your hands get transferred during the countless times you touch your face each day.
- Switch your brand of soap, shampoo, makeup, or shaving cream—you may have an allergic reaction to a certain brand.
- Change your diet. Every person's body reacts differently to different foods, but common culprits are greasy and sugary foods. Research has shown that eating chocolate doesn't affect acne (where do you volunteer for this kind of experiment?).
- Get some sun (but not too much—skin cancer isn't fun, either).
- Work out to relieve stress. Some people break out when they're under pressure.
- Try an over-the-counter medication. You may have to experiment with a few brands to find the one that works best. This stuff is expensive, so if you're unsuccessful after a few trips to the drugstore, you may save yourself money in the long run by visiting a dermatologist.
- Wait awhile. Most people leave their acne with their adolescence.

Extra Help   If your acne doesn't respond to these treatments, a dermatologist may be able to help. Dermatologists have an arsenal of weapons, including acetone, high-power ointments, internal medicines (including birth control pills for women), and ultraviolet radiation. And head transplants (just kidding).

◆

14. What is cellulite?

Most physicians will tell you that there's no such thing. People point to their behinds and say, "Explain this!" So doctors explain that there is no unique name for fat when it occurs in particular places. Fat is fat.

Women tend to store fat around their thighs and rears; men get wider in the abdomen. But the only way to get rid of any fat, regardless of your sex, is by following a healthy diet and getting plenty of exercise. Other "cures" are fiction.

◆

15. Is sunbathing dangerous?

Most teenagers figure they're too young to worry about skin cancer (you're not). The catch is, skin damage is *cumulative* —if you get too many exposure "demerits" now, you'll pay later when your skin can't take it anymore. In other words, it's burn now, fry later.

Most skin cancer is curable. The really deadly melanomas are 90 percent curable if detected early. But nearly 8,500 people die each year from skin cancer.

If you sunburn easily and don't tan, have fair skin, red or blond hair, and light-colored eyes, you are at higher risk. If you had a severe blistering burn as a child, you are at greater risk. Ten percent of skin cancers run in the family.

So, watch your skin. Wear sunscreen: experts recommend

at least 15 SPF (sun protection factor). And get yourself a cool-looking hat.

◆

16. What hairstyle is best for you?

Obviously, it's the one that makes you say, "Yes!" when you look in the mirror. *Finding* that look is the tricky part. Start with your face. If it's long and thin or rectangular (in an up-and-down way), you may want to add fullness to the sides. If you have a round or square face, you should minimize the sides.

Stylists can be extremely helpful in determining the right cut for you. They should consider the shape of your face, the kind of hair you have, how handy you are with it, and your life-style. It won't do you any good to get a great cut that requires a lot of care if all you want is a wash and wear.

A couple of warnings about stylists. Some are truly fad crazy, so if she wants to do something wild and doesn't consider some of the above points, you may not be happy with the results (and the stuff is hard to glue back). You may not get the best results with a new style at some "discount" salons. If you decide to keep the new style, a less-expensive salon may be just fine for future visits.

◆

17. How do you pick the right eyeglass frames?

The right pair of frames can make you look smarter or more handsome or anything you want. The wrong pair can seal your membership in the nerd club. Here are some general rules to follow:

- The frame color should harmonize with your hair color.
- The shape should softly follow the shape of your face.
- They shouldn't emphasize a pronounced facial contour.

For example, avoid square frames if you have a square jaw; squarish frames with rounded edges will look better.

- Proportion your glasses to the size of your face and keep the width the same as your temples.
- Make sure that the frames don't go too far down your cheeks or your face will look droopy.
- The top of the frames should be even with your eyebrows or higher.
- Avoid frames that come with a built-in nose and mustache.

Actually, the *best* thing to do is to take along a friend with good taste who's not afraid to tell you what looks good—and what looks goofy.

———————— ◆ ————————

18. Can a tattoo be removed?

Yes, but it's pretty expensive, and the procedure probably will cause damage. If the tattoo is small, it can be removed surgically. If the tattoo is large or in a sensitive place, it may be removed by laser. This process is more expensive—$300 to $800. A surgical dermatologist or plastic surgeon may perform the procedure.

Anything that cuts into the skin is likely to cause damage in the form of a disfiguring scar. So before you get that flamboyant fish emblazoned on your tush, consider what it will take to throw it back.

———————— ◆ ————————

19. Who decides what's going to be popular?

They do. And *they* never tell *anyone* what's going to be popular until it is. *Anyone* is pretty ticked because he's always out of style and *they* won't talk to him. It's a vicious cycle.

—— BODY ——

20. How do you catch AIDS?
21. What can you do about bad breath?
22. How can you tell if sex organs are "normal size"?
23. What's normal development for men?
24. What's normal development for women?
25. What can you do about a problem with too much gas?
26. How can people with no money and no insurance get emergency medical care?
27. How can you get a good night's sleep?
28. Does eating an apple a day really help?
29. What's the best way to deal with body odor?
30. How much sleep do you need?
31. Why do scabs itch? Is it safe to pick them?
32. Is chicken soup really a cure for a cold?
33. Why do some people tend to attract mosquitoes?
34. What causes headaches?
35. Why does your nose run when you cry?
36. What's the most abused organ of a teenager's body?
37. How fast does hair grow?
38. How many hairs are there on the human head?
39. If you're choking, is it possible to perform the Heimlich maneuver on yourself?
40. Do you have to get any shots after childhood?
41. When should you get a Pap smear?
42. Are there any warning signs for cancer?
43. With air bags and crash-tested cars, do seat belts make much of a difference?
44. Are bicycle helmets important?
45. Can laughing improve your health?

20. How do you catch AIDS?

HIV (the AIDS virus) travels from one body to the other via blood or semen. Drug users can trade the virus if they share the same needle. The most common way the virus gets into the body is through sex. If your infected partner's blood or semen gets into your bloodstream, you're exposed. You don't have to have an open sore to transfer the virus: people's sex organs have tiny tears in the tissue that are big enough for the virus to slip through.

◆

21. What can you do about bad breath?

Halitosis (smells like it sounds) usually comes from having mouth sores, bad teeth, infected gums, or stomach problems, or brushing your teeth with anchovy paste. Going without eating can give you bad breath, too. With no food to process, your saliva stagnates. That's one reason why eating, drinking, chewing gum, or having a Certs encounter can help—the new saliva runs your mouth through the rinse cycle. Of course, brushing and flossing help, too.

Smoking causes bad breath partly because your mouth smells like an ashtray and partly because it messes up the bacteria in your mouth and thickens the lining of your mouth and tongue. These problems go away as soon as you stop smoking.

Lots of people who are good at brushing their teeth forget to clean the rest of the mouth while they're in there. Every so often use a soft brush to clean the other surfaces—gums, tongue, cheeks (but leave that punching bag alone). If you brush only your teeth, it's like washing the car windows but not the car.

Mouthwash is pretty much of a temporary fix—it doesn't wash away all the smelly stuff any more than rain cleans all the dirt off your car.

If keeping your mouth clean and active doesn't seem to help the problem, ask your dentist about it on your next visit. If the culprit is gum disease, he or she can treat the problem and save you a bundle in breath mints.

◆

22. How can you tell if sex organs are "normal size"?

Like other body parts, these come in plenty of shapes and sizes. The good news is that size has almost *nothing* to do with pleasure (God may have a sense of humor, but He's not cruel). He also may not be finished with you yet. Your body is still growing and changing and not everything develops at the same rate.

If you're concerned that you're not developing according to plan, talk to your doctor, who's probably been asked the same question by several other patients that week and knows how to deal with it.

◆

23. What's normal development for men?

Puberty usually takes place between eleven and fifteen years of age, sometimes earlier, sometimes later. It can be argued that "late bloomers" actually have more satisfying sex lives because the earlier one starts having sex, the greater his chances of developing sexual problems later on.

Penis size varies a lot. One of the lesser-known occurrences of Murphy's Law is that most of the guys in your gym class will look "normal"; you'll think you're too small, too big, or shaped "wrong." (They're thinking the same thing about themselves.) The nerve endings in a woman's vagina are concentrated at the opening, so shape and size don't make much of a difference.

It's normal to have unexpected erections connected with

no erotic thought. The only thing you can count on (Murphy's Law again) is that they will occur at the most potentially embarrassing moments.

It's normal to have one testicle larger than the other. It's normal for your organs to all but disappear when you jump into freezing water. It's normal to have your breasts grow a little bit; this goes away after a while.

It's normal for the sex organs to develop before pubic hair develops; the reverse is also normal. They seem to use different calendars.

———————— ◆ ————————

24. What's normal development for women?

Girls generally experience menarche (first menstruation) between nine and eighteen years of age; the average age is about thirteen. Athletes often start their first period later than their less active friends.

Other signs of puberty can occur before or after your first period. Pubic hair develops sometimes before, sometimes after, the sex organs. Breasts are more like fraternal than identical twins: they grow at different rates and sometimes end up being slightly uneven in size.

———————— ◆ ————————

25. What can you do about a problem with too much gas?

This embarrassing problem would be even funnier if it weren't so painful. Here are a few things you can do:

Change Your Diet   Foods that produce a lot of gas include certain kinds of vegetables, beans, and fruits. Your body may react to other foods—figure out which ones and avoid them, especially prior to a date.

Spit Out Your Gum   Gum chewing causes you to swallow air.

Go Now   If you're near a bathroom when you first feel the need to go, do it. Lots of folks create unneccesary problems because they wait until they're back home in familiar territory.

Move to Sea Level   Problems with gas are more acute the higher the elevation. In high-elevation cities, people at social gatherings step outside periodically to "stretch their legs."

See a Doctor   Sometimes too much gas means there's something wrong with your system. A physician can help you figure out the problem and the treatment.

———————— ◆ ————————

26. How can people with no money and no insurance get emergency medical care?

A hospital *must* admit you if you have a life-threatening ailment that requires immediate treatment—regardless of your financial state. After you are stabilized, you may end up being transferred to a government-funded (e.g., city or county) hospital.

This *doesn't* mean that the hospital won't try to collect on the bill you ran up in the emergency room. If you can't pay the whole bill, the hospital will try to get you to pay a percentage. Children under five have a better deal because they're covered by a government insurance program called Medicaid (in some states, the age is higher).

People without the means to pay for emergency treatment usually try to get to a city or county hospital where the fees are lower than those of a private hospital. In urban areas these public hospitals receive most of the gunshot and stabbing cases, so if you're in there for something "minor," such as a broken bone, you may have to wait in line.

———————— ◆ ————————

27. How can you get a good night's sleep?

Some people are unconscious the moment they hit the pillow, then they sleep through cat fights and earthquakes until the alarm goes off the next morning. But most of us aren't so skilled at slumber; we need help. Here are several suggestions from sleep specialists:

Before Bed

Unwind your mind. If you've had a nonstop day—from school to practice to library to work—your brain hasn't had time to talk to you about anything but what you've been doing. If you go straight to bed, your mind says, "Finally! A chance to chat!" and starts telling you about who you forgot to call, what you've got to do tomorrow, where you left that bag of ripe gym clothes, and a hundred other things. Take thirty minutes to let it talk itself out.

Write it down. If there are things you have to remember for the morning, write them down and forget about them till tomorrow. (A pen and pad of paper on the nightstand can help if ideas pop into your head after you hop in the sack.)

Stay off drugs. Caffeine, sugar, alcohol, and nicotine all interfere with sleep. For example, caffeine from coffee, tea, or cola drunk up to four hours before bed can mess with your bed head.

Check the temp. Most people sleep best when the room temperature is 60° to 65°F.

In Bed

Relax. Progressively relax each muscle area, starting at your toes and working slowly up to your head.

Show your body who's boss. Don't go to bed until you're sleepy. If you don't fall asleep in twenty minutes, get up and don't lie down again until you're good and sleepy.

Get in a rut. Try to go to sleep at the same time each night and get up at the same time each morning (no matter when you went to sleep).

(If you're reading this in bed, put down the book and go to sleep.)

———————— ◆ ————————

28. Does eating an apple a day really help?

Yep. Fruits and vegetables contain stuff your body needs to stay healthy now and to fend off nasty things like cancer and heart disease later on. If you've been skipping through the garden instead of eating from it, you're not alone: 90 percent of Americans eat only *half* the amount recommended by the Food and Drug Administration.

If you want to change your ways, start small and work up from there. If you're like most people, just eating one piece of fruit a day will be a drastic improvement. Add a salad each day, then a green vegetable or two. (If you bury the peas in the mashed potatoes, you'll hardly know they're there.) The goal? At least five servings of fruits and vegetables a day.[1]

———————— ◆ ————————

29. What's the best way to deal with body odor?

One of the downsides of puberty is that your body becomes a factory of unflattering scents. The biggest problem is your armpits, which advertisers delicately call underarms. In case you haven't peeked, it's generally pretty dark, warm, and wet under there—a bacteria breeder's bonanza. The odor is actually a blend of your body's "scent" (musk if you prefer) and the smell of the bacteria.

Deodorants are chemicals that work to take away this odor. If you don't drown in sweat but still smell like a locker room, this stuff is for you.

Antiperspirants are chemicals that try to stop your body from sweating. With some bodies, that's an uphill battle. If you get wet circles under your arms just trying to get your locker open, you should try an antiperspirant.

If you have both problems, get a brand that includes both types of ingredients.

Everyone's body chemistry is different, so the brand that works for someone else may not work for you. Shop around until you find the right formula. If nothing seems to work, check your jacket pocket: the odor may not be you but the tuna sandwich you left there last May.

------------◆------------

30. How much sleep do you need?

Everyone is different. Some people do well on five hours; others need ten or more. For example, Thomas Edison did pretty well on four hours of sleep each night; Albert Einstein required twelve (which may explain his hair).

The best way to find out what you need is to experiment. Choose a wake-up time, then try going to bed at different hours each night for a week. Too little sleep will make you tired and cranky. Too *much* sleep can do the same thing, so you have to shoot for the happy medium.

By the way, the older you get, the less sleep you need. People in their seventies and eighties often get by on four hours because the body doesn't need to spend all night regenerating itself.

------------◆------------

31. Why do scabs itch? Is it safe to pick them?

The scab isn't itching—it's the skin underneath that's the problem. As a wound heals, the nerves begin to work again and send signals to the brain expressing discomfort. (Itch is one of the friendliest members of the Pain family: its meaner siblings include Burn, Prickle, Rip, Throb, and Nausea.)

As for picking, let's face it: it's lots of fun. But the scab is a natural bandage that should be removed by the one who put it there. Sometimes picking at a scab can create a scar.

◆

32. Is chicken soup really a cure for a cold?

There's still no cure for the cold. However, hot drinks generally increase the flow of nasal secretions and alleviate cold symptoms. The taste and aroma may have a placebo effect, especially if you've always been told that the soup will cure you. Your body also may respond to the vitamins and minerals from the vegetables and chicken bones that were boiled to make the broth.

◆

33. Why do some people tend to attract mosquitoes?

Popularity does have its downside. Mosquitoes are attracted to certain chemicals in the blood, the amounts of which vary from person to person and from day to day with the same person (especially women, whose menstrual cycles rearrange their blood chemistry). In other words, some people have tastier blood.

Mosquitoes are also attracted to warmth and moisture, so if

you're the wettest and warmest person in a group, you may be elected most popular. If you're someone mosquitoes find attractive, stick to repellent. There's no scientific proof of the effectiveness of natural body repellents such as loading up on vitamins, garlic, or mustard.[2]

34. What causes headaches?

Most headaches occur when the tissue surrounding your brain is stretched from too much blood pressure. The brain itself doesn't have pain sensors (it has enough to think about already). Common causes include irregular meals, too much excitement, extreme noise, exhaustion, loud music, food additives, and head jarring.

35. Why does your nose run when you cry?

Your eyes have a built-in wash system. The tear ducts produce fluid that washes your eyes and keeps them moist. The dirty fluid is drained off to your nose via the nasolacrimal duct.

When you cry, the eye produces more fluid than can trickle down the drainpipe: some of it spills down your cheek. The fluid that does get drained out the nasolacrimal duct ends up in your nose in amounts that cause you to sniffle.

36. What's the most abused organ of a teenager's body?

The skin. Most students think it's just a wrapper for the rest of the body, but it's an important part of the system itself.

Its functions include protection from injury, sunlight, and bacteria. It contains a fatty substance that makes the skin waterproof, and it has sensors to detect touch, pain, and temperature. It helps maintain body temperature, producing sweat when it's hot and closing the blood vessels in the skin when it's cold, conserving heat for other organs.

How to Treat Skin Right

- Put on sunscreen. It isn't just to keep you from hurting or peeling. Sunscreen protects your skin from damage that may not show up for decades, including deadly and expensive cancers and growths.
- Wash your face. Puberty causes the sebaceous glands in your face to produce too much oil. Oil that's trapped by dirt causes infections (acne).
- Wash everywhere else. Puberty also increases body hair and sweating, which means more places for bacteria to grow. Keep your skin clean in these areas by washing with soap and water and drying thoroughly.
- Protect yourself. Wear knee pads, elbow pads, and a helmet whenever you're doing a sport that can skin you up. Your skin is losing its ability to heal itself instantly without scarring.

─────────── ◆ ───────────

37. How fast does hair grow?

Some people's hair grows faster than others, but an average is about one millimeter every three days. That comes to an inch every two and a half months. If you have a crew cut now and want hair halfway down your back, stay away from the barber for at least three years.

─────────── ◆ ───────────

38. How many hairs are there on the human head?

You have about 300,000 hairs on your scalp. Of those, about 100 to 150 are shed each day. (That's what clogs up your shower drain, especially during finals week.) What's more, about every three years each hair follicle goes on sabbatical— it takes three months off and doesn't try to grow any hair.

◆

39. If you're choking, is it possible to perform the Heimlich maneuver on yourself?

No, but don't despair—there is another way. If you're by yourself, dive onto the back of the nearest hardback chair or couch so that you strike it with your upper abdomen, just below your ribs. That should dislodge the offending piece.

◆

40. Do you have to get any shots after childhood?

Unfortunately, you may need a few more shots in your lifetime. You should have a diphtheria and tetanus booster every ten years. You may also need one last booster for measles. If you are sexually active, a vaccine for hepatitis B is recommended. Flu shots and pneumonia shots are really for high-risk or older people, so tell your parents to get them.[3]

If you're traveling out of the country, you may need a bunch of shots, but your doctor should know all about the ones you need for wherever you're going.

◆

41. When should you get a Pap smear?

Women, if you are over eighteen or you've had sex, an annual pelvic exam and Pap smear are recommended. Pap smears detect cervical cancer, which has no symptoms in its early stages. This cancer is now almost 100 percent curable if diagnosed early and treated promptly. A few moments of small discomfort may save your life.

◆

42. Are there any warning signs for cancer?

Here's a cute little memorization trick from the medical faculty at the University of California, Los Angeles:

C Change in bowel or bladder movements
A A sore or scab that refuses to heal
U Unusual bleeding or discharge
T Thickening or lump in breast or elsewhere
I Indigestion or difficulty swallowing
O Obvious change in wart or mole
N Nagging cough or hoarseness

Don't wait for symptoms to become uncomfortable or painful; pain isn't usually an early symptom of cancer.

◆

43. With air bags and crash-tested cars, do seat belts make much of a difference?

Decide for yourself.

- Most cars still don't have air bags.
- Air bags protect only in front-end collisions; most people are hit in the rear or side.
- More than half the people killed in car crashes would be alive if they'd worn their seat belts. (They'd make great spokespeople except that they're dead.)
- Eighty percent of fatal accidents occur at speeds under 40 mph.
- Without a seat belt, if you drive into a solid object at 30 mph, your body will hit the windshield with the same force that you'd hit the ground with if you fell from a five-story building.
- You're twenty-five to forty times more likely to be killed in an accident if you're thrown from the car.
- People wearing seat belts in a car fire or when trapped underwater survive more often than those not wearing them because they're less likely to be knocked unconscious in the crash that got them there.[4]

By the way, a shoulder belt shouldn't be worn without a lap belt because it will strangle you on impact. If your car automatically buckles your shoulders, remember to buckle your lap belt.

———————— ◆ ————————

44. Are bicycle helmets important?

They're funny looking. They're slightly uncomfortable. They save your life. On the road or off-road, they're a smart idea.

- Approximately 125,000 cyclists suffer from head injuries each year.
- Approximately 850 cyclists each year die from accidents —75 percent suffered head injuries.
- Low-speed crashes—5 mph or less—can result in permanent brain damage.
- Helmets would reduce head injuries by 85 percent and fatalities by 50 percent.

People who ride off-road without a helmet are *completely* stupid. If you go mountain biking with a friend who won't wear one, tell him that. Tell him you won't enjoy spoon-feeding him when he bashes.

◆

45. Can laughing improve your health?

Some studies have shown that people who use laughter as a coping device have higher levels of infection-fighting antibodies. A study from Duke University showed that laughter may reduce the risk of heart attacks by diffusing anger.

On average, young children laugh up to five hundred times a day while adults laugh only fifteen times in that same day.[5] You're probably somewhere in the middle but headed for the low number all too fast.

To prevent any further drop in your laugh factor, take action now. Make time for humor each day. Hang out with people who make you laugh, and make them laugh, too.

CHEMICALS

46. What's the difference between crack and regular cocaine?
47. Why isn't marijuana legal?
48. Why do some people die from cocaine use?
49. How can some people get drunk on just one beer?
50. How can a person get sober in a hurry?
51. How do you tell if someone is an alcoholic?
52. What do you do about a parent who has a drug or an alcohol problem?

46. What's the difference between crack and regular cocaine?

Cocaine   It is an expensive white powder that's either inhaled or injected. It takes away your appetite, increases your heart and breathing rates, and gives you a runny nose. The high lasts about twenty minutes, usually followed by severe depression.

Crack   It is more addictive and less expensive (if you count your life cheap) than cocaine, which it's derived from. It comes in white or tan pellets that are smoked through a glass pipe (which produces a crackling sound—hence the name). Crack smoking takes away the appetite, increases the heart and breathing rates, and raises body temperature. The high lasts from three to ten minutes, but the depression afterward is so severe that some people smoke it not for the euphoria itself but to escape the crash. It's a drug dealer's dream.

———————◆———————

47. Why isn't marijuana legal?

For   The argument for legalization goes something like this: if we legalize marijuana use, the allure attached to doing something illegal would disappear. Selling the drug through stores would put drug dealers out of work or at least take a big bite out of their business. For example, organized crime's connection with alcohol dried up when the Prohibition laws were repealed in 1933.

Millions of dollars in government money could go toward fighting "serious" drugs instead of being wasted on discovering, arresting, prosecuting, and incarcerating marijuana growers, smugglers, and dealers. The government could even *make* money with a "sin tax" like the one charged on tobacco products.

Against   The argument against legalization is pretty simple. Although the end of Prohibition shut down the criminal trade in alcohol, it didn't stop the criminals. Many just switched to peddling other drugs such as cocaine, heroin, and marijuana. It's doubtful that drug dealers who lose one product line are going to quit the business: it's easier just to switch products. (When a grocer runs out of apples, he doesn't close the store—he just sells more oranges.)

The economics of legalization are suspect, too. The savings to the criminal justice system plus the tax revenues from alcohol don't even begin to cover the economic burden that alcohol abuse causes. Half a million people each year are treated for serious injuries from alcohol-related accidents— that's a big hospital bill. Then there are the costs of the cars and property destroyed by drunk drivers; medical bills for treating alcoholics; loss of worker productivity; families impoverished by a parent whose life has been destroyed by drinking.

If legalizing marijuana would increase its use, the price of abuse would also rise.

———————— ◆ ————————

48. Why do some people die from cocaine use?

Cocaine is a stimulant: it "revs your engine" by increasing your heart and breathing rates. Like a car engine, your body's engine can take only so much of this before it burns out. A cocaine overdose blows your engine: your heart or lungs stop working.

Cocaine users like to think that they can prevent this by limiting the number of times they rev their engine. But they use a very unreliable fuel. Dealers dilute the drug with other white powders such as baking soda to increase the amount of product for sale. The amount of pure cocaine differs from one batch to the next, and it's not easy to tell what the mix is (cocaine isn't sold with a label). If you're accustomed to sniffing stuff that's pretty "watered down" and you get ahold of a much purer batch, you may not realize it until it's too late.

Some people think the very worst that can happen is that they will start to overdose, their friends will rush them to the hospital, and the doctors will stick a magic formula into them that will bring them out of it. WRONG. Unlike a heroin overdose, which can often be stopped with an injection, with cocaine there's no turning back. Your system has gone haywire, and there's little anyone can do about it.

In other words, your engine is racing out of control, there's no one in the driver's seat, and the doors are locked. Doctors don't have keys to get in and shut you down before you die.

◆

49. How can some people get drunk on just one beer?

The biggest factor affecting drunkenness is your body's weight. A smaller body means less blood and tissue to absorb the alcohol. Here's a chart showing the level of alcohol in people of different weights within an hour of drinking beer. The numbers refer to blood alcohol concentration (BAC), which is the percentage of pure alcohol in your blood. A BAC of .10 means the blood is 10% alcohol.

Other things influence how alcohol affects you, including body chemistry, how fast you drink, your mood, and the amount of food in your stomach. A small person with no alcohol tolerance and an empty stomach can easily have a

BAC of .06 after just one beer. In some states, that's enough to get arrested.

Blood Alcohol Concentration and Body Weight

Weight	Number of 12-Ounce Beers				
	1	**2**	**3**	**4**	**5**
100	.04	.09	.15	.20	.25
120	.03	.08	.12	.16	.21
140	.02	.06	.10	.14	.18
160	.02	.05	.09	.12	.15
180	.02	.05	.08	.10	.13
200	.01	.04	.07	.09	.12

0–.04:   Not legally drunk, but impairment is possible.

.05–.09:   State laws vary; mental and physical impairment is noticeable.

.10 and above: Presumed intoxicated in all states.

◆

50. How can a person get sober in a hurry?

You can't. Your blood alcohol concentration drops at a rate of .015 per hour if you have no more drinks. With a little math (get out your calculator) you can figure out that if you have a BAC of .10 (i.e., you're drunk), it'll take you three hours to get to .05, which is still not good. You won't have all the alcohol out of you for another three hours.

The slowpoke to sobriety is your liver. It's the only organ that processes alcohol, and it takes its sweet time doing it. You can run in place in a cold shower while drinking ten cups of coffee, and your liver still won't work any faster. Livers are like that.

What does the coffee do? It takes away some of the *sleepiness* that can come from a depressant such as alcohol. You may not fall asleep, but you'll still be drunk.

———————— ◆ ————————

51. How do you tell if someone is an alcoholic?

Alcoholics *need* to drink. They can go for a time without drinking, but in the end, they need a drink to keep life satisfying or at least survivable. They typically develop a high tolerance for alcohol, which means they can have a few drinks without appearing drunk. In fact, drunkenness isn't always a symptom: someone can be addicted to alcohol without ever appearing drunk.

Other Possible Signs

- Mood changes
- Personality changes
- Denial of any problem
- Drinking in the morning
- Drinking alone

———————— ◆ ————————

52. What do you do about a parent who has a drug or an alcohol problem?

If ever there was a situation specifically designed to drive you crazy, this is it. You can try to dismiss or ignore the problem. You can try to run away from the problem. You can try to take care of it by keeping the family functioning. But the problem doesn't go away.

You love your parent, but you can't help feeling this incredible amount of anger for what he or she has done to the family. Then you feel guilty for having such ugly thoughts about a person you're supposed to love. It's a nightmare. Here are a few things you can do:

Start Talking   Discuss your feelings with the other parent, a trusted adult, or a counselor. This person can help you decide on a plan of action, including how you will behave around the afflicted parent. At some point, you'll need to discuss your feelings with the afflicted parent, too.

Set Limits   This is a strange thing to do with a parent. Carefully decide what you will and won't do in the presence of your afflicted parent when he or she has been using or drinking. For example, you have the right to say, "I won't ride in the car with you." Too often children of troubled parents try to make everything okay. It's *not* okay, and it's *not* your responsibility to fix it all.

Find Support   Families of alcoholics are strange beasts. People from these kinds of families often get together for support, encouragement, and advice. Such a group probably meets in your area. Al-Anon and Adult Children of Alcoholics are two such groups—you can find their numbers by looking in the phone book or by calling the local office of Alcoholics Anonymous.

COLLEGE

53. What can you do to improve your SAT score?
54. How can you tell if the SAT prep course you choose is going to help?
55. Does the school you go to really affect your job future?
56. How do you choose a major?
57. What are fraternities and sororities?
58. Some people say fraternities and sororities are the best thing about college; others say they're dumb. Who's right?
59. Is college ever a waste of time?
60. How do you come up with the money for college?

53. What can you do to improve your SAT score?

1. Retrieve your copy of *Taking the SAT* that was sent to you in the mail when you registered for the test. Review the book—it contains sample questions and test-taking strategies.

2. Get prepped. Several classes out there can prepare you for the SAT. These courses *can* make a difference, often with an 80- to 160-point improvement. Math scores rise more than verbal scores.[1]

3. Retake the test. You may take it as many times as you like and pick and choose the two scores you like the best. Your score will be boosted by an average of 40 points each time you retake the test.[2]

4. Rest. Eat well, and get plenty of sleep the night before the test.

5. Fuel up. Eat a sensible, sugarless breakfast, and allow yourself some time to wake up and get ready.

6. Have fun a few days beforehand. You probably won't benefit by cramming right up till the day of the test. Take time to play but don't stay out too late.

7. Have your stuff ready to go the night before. You need to bring several #2 pencils and your ID, or you don't get to join in all the fun.

◆

54. How can you tell if the SAT prep course you choose is going to help?

The competition to get into college has made SAT preparation a multimillion-dollar business. Here's a quick checklist to help you find a course or book that will do the most for you:

1. Does the method teach you how the SAT is structured and scored?
2. Does it teach test-taking skills you can absorb in a few weeks? Such a skill might be to gain familiarity with the directions so you don't have to waste time on test day.
3. Does it include questions from real SATs? A book's copyright page will tell you.
4. Can it target strengths and weaknesses?
5. Does it contain an unrealistically long vocabulary list of thousands of words?
6. For a book, is it easy to understand, written in plain language, and not frighteningly thick?
7. For a course, what is its track record? Ask what percentage of students increase their scores and by how much—and whether independent studies verify score gains.
8. What guarantees does the course offer? Not many will refund your money, but some promise to work with you until you are satisfied with your score gains.[3]

◆

55. Does the school you go to really affect your job future?

It depends on the job. Some employers put a lot of weight on your alma mater. For example, big accounting firms may not hire you if your school isn't on their list. If you have your heart set on a certain career, ask adults in that business if the school you attend will make a critical difference in your hireability.

Hiring someone on the basis of the college he attended seems an awful lot like judging a person by his brand of clothing. But the quality of teaching varies widely from college to college—some colleges give out diplomas to students who can barely read and write. The quality of education also varies from department to department within the same school. A school with a nationally respected education department may have a mediocre business department.

An employer who's met graduates from many schools knows that certain colleges tend to turn out certain kinds of workers. Choosing who to hire is always a gamble: hiring someone from a good school is one way of improving the odds.

◆

56. How do you choose a major?

The average college student changes his or her major six times before graduating. Here are the five most popular methods for choosing:

1. Use a dart board.
2. Let your parents pick.
3. Choose the one that your friends have picked so you'll always have someone to take notes for you when you skip class.
4. Pick the major that will set you up in the career that will make you the most money. (Then switch majors when you discover that no salary is big enough to compensate you for performing a job you do not enjoy. Tip: try to discover this before you graduate.)
5. Choose a major in an area for which you have a passion. You'll spend most of your first two years taking general education courses. Use these classes to discover a passion and consider pursuing a major in that area. College provides you with a plethora, myriad, cornucopia (you took the SAT so you know what these words mean) of subjects not offered in high school. Explore a few of them before you make your final choice.

For most jobs, it's the degree that matters and not your area of study. Apart from doctors, scientists, and engineers, most people work outside their specific major. (If you're planning to be a doctor, your patients will prefer a premed background to a degree in medieval history.)

When you've chosen your major, don't be afraid to change your mind. After all, there's that average to maintain.

———————— ◆ ————————

57. What are fraternities and sororities?

Some young urban children asked a social worker, "What's a fraternity?" Putting it in terms they'd understand, she replied, "A fraternity is a gang for older white boys." And if you take away the violence associated with gangs, the comparison is pretty accurate.

Like a gang, a fraternity (for men) or a sorority (for women) provides its members with fellowship, tradition, and the security of belonging to something special. There are initiations and rituals and secret handshakes passed down from one class to the next. Membership in a Greek society is exclusive. New recruits (called pledges) must be invited by an older member, and they must pass an initiation that typically includes an evaluation of their character and some kind of ritual that ranges from solemn to silly. While it is illegal to discriminate, many Greek societies tend to be racially segregated.

The popularity of fraternities and sororities varies from one college to another and from region to region. They're especially popular on southern and midwestern campuses, much less so in the West.

———————— ◆ ————————

58. Some people say fraternities and sororities are the best thing about college; others say they're dumb. Who's right?

Everyone. Your experience with a Greek society depends on the people in it (they tend to attract people of similar lifestyles and values). If your house is made up of superficial people preoccupied with parties—and you're not—college life is going to get old real fast.

What Can Be Good about a Greek Society Lots of social gatherings, sense of belonging and tradition, prestige, some accountability, occasional opportunities to do good works in the community.

What Can Be Bad about a Greek Society Too much partying, lots of alcohol, little ethnic and cultural diversity, seen as juvenile.

---

59. Is college ever a waste of time?

You hear stories about college graduates who toil four years to earn a degree, then discover that the only jobs they can find are ones that don't require a college degree: checkout clerk, bus driver, construction worker. It happens.

The reasons vary. If the national or regional economy is slow, or a particular market is slow, people may not be hiring. If the student picked a major that's too popular, the colleges may be graduating more candidates than there are positions available (supply and demand). If the graduate got a good education, he or she will eventually be able to find a job with rewards that justify the time in college.

If, however, the graduate was one of the many people who

somehow slipped through college without learning much, it might be a waste.

So what's the answer to the question? Yes, college can be a waste of time but only if you let it. The choice is up to you. By the way, financial figures support this: college graduates average lifetime earnings of $500,000 greater than those without degrees.

◆

60. How do you come up with the money for college?

Basically, you can look for it in four places (five if you count winning the lottery).

You and Your Family Your savings account, income from part-time and summer jobs, money your parents provide, gifts from your rich uncle—all are possible sources.

Loans Government subsidized loans are ones that you don't have to repay until after you graduate. Stafford Loans (also known as Guaranteed Student Loans) are made through banks; the government guarantees to pay back the bank if you fail to repay the loan. Perkins Loans are for needier students; they're a lot like Stafford Loans, but they have a lower interest rate.

Grants A grant is government money that you don't have to pay back. Pell Grants and Supplemental Educational Opportunity Grants come from the federal government; state governments also provide grants.

Scholarships Money is available from schools, corporations, and other organizations that you don't have to pay back. Churches, community groups, religious organizations, and labor unions also offer scholarships. Ask around.

Unless you and your family can come up with all the money, you'll need to apply for funding through the other sources. To do this, you have to fill out a Financial Aid Form (FAF) or Family Financial Statement (FFS) that details your own and your family's finances. You can pick up one of these forms from your school's guidance counselor. Whenever you apply for money, an organization will need a copy of this form.

Your guidance counselor can also give you the application details for the various loans, grants, and scholarships available to you. Most money sources have application deadlines: miss the date and you miss out on a chance to get the money.

The final place to look for money is the college itself. Administrators will want to know that you've exhausted every other source before they consider you for their scholarships.

COMMUNICATION

61. How do you keep from getting nervous when giving a speech?
62. When is it okay to break rules of grammar?
63. How can you improve your writing *without* taking a writing class?
64. How can you break a word habit such as cussing or saying "um" or "like"?
65. How can you break the habit of gossiping?
66. How do you stop people from gossiping about you?
67. What's wrong with tuna fish?
68. What are some cool-sounding words you can use to make yourself appear more interesting?

61. How do you keep from getting nervous when giving a speech?

Virtually everyone experiences some kind of anxiety just before speaking or performing in front of a crowd (some are just better at hiding it). Here are some tricks people use to get through it:

Beforehand

- Do something physical. Run up and down a flight of stairs. Do fifty jumping jacks. The exercise releases tension and makes you feel better.

- Recruit a cheerleader. Ask a friend to sit beside you before you go up. Have her check you out—hair right, collar straight, face devoid of lunch leftovers, and so on. Let her tell you how great you'll be.

During

- Memorize your first thirty seconds so well that you can deliver the material smoothly and brilliantly without much thought. You're most likely to stumble at this point, so be safe and pave the way.

- Look at your audience and smile. There's only one thing scarier than looking out on an audience: it's *not* looking at them and imagining all those eyes staring back at you.

- Get a reaction. As soon as possible, give the audience a chance to respond to you: a show of hands, applause, laughter, or answers to a question. The feedback convinces your skeptical and chicken-hearted nerves that those people out there are friendly and really do want to hear what you have to say. (Audience response also makes any speech better.)

- Find friendly faces. As you speak, look for a few people in the audience who seem especially interested. Let your eyes return to these faces every so often—their silent feedback cheers you on.

◆

62. When is it okay to break rules of grammar?

When most teachers grade your writing, they do so with the aim of preparing you for college: research papers, reports, footnotes, bibliographies, and all that stuff. The rules they follow are the formal ones you find in academic and scientific writing.

In case you haven't noticed, most academic and scientific writing is . . . well, dull. In just about any other world—journalism, television, advertising, even business—you'd get fired for writing like that.

Some things that are taboo in academic writing are acceptable in other places because they make the writing more readable. Here are a few rules you can break if you're careful:

End a sentence with a preposition. In some sentences a preposition is the best ending you can think of. You know what I'm talking about. It's more casual than redoing the sentence just to match the rule: "You know of what I speak."

Start a sentence with **and.** One of your goals is to get the reader from the first sentence to the last via all the sentences in between. If the reader drops out somewhere in the middle of your piece, you've failed. Every so often you can use an *and* to entice a reader from one sentence to the next. And it works.

Use an incomplete sentence for effect. Really.

———————— ◆ ————————

63. How can you improve your writing *without* taking a writing class?

Three ways.

Write short sentences. Short ones are easier to write and quicker to read.

Write in active voice. Don't say, "The creation of the monster was by Dr. Frankenstein." Say, "Dr. Frankenstein created the monster."

Write with nouns and verbs. Lazy writers create word pictures with adjectives and adverbs. Good writers make the nouns and verbs convey the image. Don't crawl slowly; *creep*. Don't run fast; *sprint.*

◆

64. How can you break a word habit such as cussing or saying "um" or "like"?

Word habits are tough to break. The word is out of your mouth before your brain can stop it. The way to break the habit is to make yourself conscious of every time you do it. Here are two proven methods:

Write it down. Every time you cuss (or say "um" or whatever it is you do that's driving you crazy), make a tally mark on a piece of paper you carry in your pocket. Just the act of marking it down is trouble enough to make repeating the habit not worth the effort. And looking at a mark-covered tally sheet at the end of the day will inspire you to do better tomorrow.

Pay a quarter. Ask your friends to help you break the habit. If they catch you saying what you're not supposed to, they can demand a quarter from you. Carry a pocketful of quarters the first couple of days to pay up. Your habits will change as you watch your money disappear.

◆

65. How can you break the habit of gossiping?

Passing gossip is a form of power—you can control what someone thinks about another. Listening to gossip is a form of prestige—it enrolls you in an exclusive class of "those who know."

But the price for this kind of power and prestige is too high. Gossip cheapens a friendship and makes it hard to establish close friends. You can do several things to break the gossip habit.

Change the subject. Reporters, talk show hosts, and people skilled at conversation are masters at turning the course of a conversation without a fuss. Everyone should learn this art.

Walk away. When you can't control the course of a conversation that turns to gossip, just make an excuse and leave.

Say, "Stop." You have the right to choose what you hear. Unfortunately, ears don't come equipped with flaps, so you have to stop the noise at the source. It's okay to say, "Please don't tell me." Eventually, people will figure out that you're not into gossip, and they won't try to involve you.

Make a pact. It's always easier to change a habit when you have a friend to do it with. Make a deal and hold each other to it.

—————————— ◆ ——————————

66. How do you stop people from gossiping about you?

The solution depends on how the gossip started. Here are the most common sources:

Payback. If you've gossiped about someone else, you're fair game for retaliation. *Solution:* don't gossip.

Envy. If you're beautiful or handsome or talented or success-ful, there will always be someone who thinks it's her job to "put you in your place." And if you happen to be arrogant, too, a bunch of people will do this. *Solutions:* (1) stay humble—the arrogant are easy marks; or (2) fail at every-thing you do so that no one can possibly envy you.

Speck of truth. Most gossip is based on *something* that's true, even if most of the story is false. If you were drunk at a party, you'll be passed out or throwing up on the geraniums by the time the story gets around. *Solution:* obviously, the wilder you are, the more mud they can spread around. Stay away from mud puddles. Live clean and treat people well.

Leaky friend. If you begin to hear your secrets bandied about school, you can be pretty sure that a friend betrayed your confidence. *Solutions:* (1) confront the friend—it might have been an accident or a misunderstanding; and (2) stop sharing secrets with friends whose confidence you're not sure of.

◆

67. What's wrong with tuna fish?

It's redundant. You don't ask for a roast beef mammal sand-wich or a turkey poultry for Thanksgiving.

Other Redundancies The U.S. Department of Redun-dancy Dept. of the United States lists these frequently com-mon repetitious redundancies of word verbiage on its list:

- Personal physician (as opposed to an impersonal doctor)
- Added bonus
- Currently ongoing
- Sierra Mountains
- Sahara Desert
- Free at no cost to you

- Each and every one
- He is a man who
- Irregardless
- General consensus
- 8 a.m. tomorrow morning

------------ ◆ ------------

68. What are some cool-sounding words you can use to make yourself appear more interesting?

Segue (SEG-way) A quick, smooth transition between things, like when a DJ says something clever between two songs. The "I had a great time tonight" from car to doorstep is the *segue* to the kiss.

Chagrin (shuh-GRIN) Embarrassment from disappointment. Let's say you like a guy, but he doesn't know it. When he finally comes up to talk to you, you're visibly thrilled. When you find out he only wants to talk about your best friend, you're *chagrined*.

Slather (SLAH-thur) To spread on thickly. If you're going to put mayonnaise on a peanut butter and jelly sandwich, you might as well *slather* it.

Soliloquy (suh-LIL-uh-kwee) A talk you give to yourself. If your little brother knocks on the door while you're talking to yourself in the mirror, say, "Leave me alone—I'm *soliloquizing*!"

DATING

69. How do you ask someone out?
70. How do you make a date more creative?
71. What do you do if you have a date planned but almost no money?
72. How do you say no to someone who asks you out?
73. What's the rule about kissing on the first date?
74. How can you make a lousy first impression?
75. What do you do if you don't want to kiss someone?
76. How do you get a member of the opposite sex to notice you?
77. Who should you ask to the prom?

69. How do you ask someone out?

This is one of the all-time scariest things to do. Here are some tips to make it a little easier:

Ask a Friend It's a lot easier to ask a friend than a semistranger you've been admiring from afar. Whenever possible, develop a friendship with someone before you try to go on a date.

Ask in Person Most guys aren't as skilled at phone conversations as girls are, so you may not come off as wonderful as you really are. Give it your best shot—and that's live and in color.

Start Casual Don't plan something elaborate or expensive on the first date. If the person doesn't know you well, she'll be scared away by all the expectations that come with it.

Double Up She's more likely to say yes if there's another couple on the date, especially if one of the people is someone she knows.

Be Specific Don't ask, "Hey, I was wondering if you might want to get together and do something sometime?" Be definite: "I'd like to take you to that movie premiere next Friday night. What do you think?"

Have a Backup Plan If she says no but gives no reason, it probably means no, I'm not interested in dating you. If she says no because she has other plans, it *may* mean that you have another chance. Ask her about Plan A. If she sounds genuinely disappointed, then you're set. Go with Plan B.

———————————— ◆ ————————————

70. How do you make a date more creative?

Life is full of routines. Dating is no exception. Most teenagers on a date go to dinner, then a movie. For variety, they go to the movie, *then* do dinner. Bust out of the rut.

Make a movie. Forget seeing one—make your own. Borrow a camcorder; write a script; take turns shooting and acting.

Jump a puddle. Go for a walk in the rain. Stand on a street corner and let drivers drench you. Stop by a playground: ride the slide, swing in the rain.

Bake a batch. Spend an hour or two in the kitchen together baking cookies for yourselves and your friends.

Pack a picnic. Make lunches and spend the day at the lake, park, or beach.

Go boating. If you can't afford a yacht, borrow someone's rubber raft and pool.

Roast marshmallows. Build a fire in a barbecue grill. Bring along the hot cocoa.

Eat cheap. Hunt for the cheapest restaurant you can find. Figure out the biggest feast you can order for $5. Bon appétit.

Play like kids again. Pick up some Play-Doh from the toy store. Make stuff.

Dress up. Each of you wears your nicest outfit for a romantic meal—at a fast-food restaurant.

———————— ◆ ————————

71. What do you do if you have a date planned but almost no money?

Here are your options:

1. Cancel the date.
2. Ask your date to pay.
3. Don't ask—just pull out an empty wallet when the dinner check comes.
4. Plan something that doesn't cost a lot of money. Consider these ideas:

   • Rent a movie (or watch one on TV).
   • Cook a meal together.
   • Go out for ice cream.
   • Attend a free concert or seminar put on by the community.
   • Go for a walk.
   • Window-shop.
   • Watch people.
   • Ride bikes.
   • See how far you can get on a city bus.

———————— ◆ ————————

72. How do you say no to someone who asks you out?

Being turned down is not on anyone's favorite pastime list. The easiest, most gentle way is to say, "Thank you for asking... but no, I don't think so." You don't have to make excuses (my cat died; I'm moving to a convent). Nor do you need to give your reason (you're a geek; I don't date losers).

If you think you may want to go out with him, but you're

not thrilled with the idea of being alone with him on a date, suggest an alternative. Ask him to join you and some of your friends at something safe and casual—a game, movie, party, trip to the beach. This approach eliminates the romantic pressure, and you get a chance to see how he behaves in public.

◆

73. What's the rule about kissing on the first date?

The rule is, do what you think is best. If you don't want to kiss, that's okay. If you do—and you sense that your date would like that, too—then kiss.

Some guys think that spending money on a girl obligates her to kiss. This idea is completely stupid. You don't buy affection.

◆

74. How can you make a lousy first impression?

If your goal is to make a *good* first impression, avoid these opening lines:

- "Are you my date?"
- "Can we hurry to the car? I don't want the neighbors to see me."
- "I've got to be back in thirty minutes."
- "Please don't talk to me tonight."
- "Please don't tell anyone we went out together."
- "Can I just have the money you plan to spend on me so I can go out by myself?"

- "Wouldn't you rather just talk on the phone?"
- "I'll be honest: I think you're a geek."
- "Can I follow you in a cab?"
- "Did you actually pay for those clothes?"
- "Can we sit at different tables?"
- "How much money do you have?"

◆

75. What do you do if you don't want to kiss someone?

Here are some time-tested kiss-avoidance tricks:*

What to Say

- "My lips are sunburned."
- "I'm feeling sick all of a sudden."
- "I just had my braces tightened."
- "The last time I kissed, I bit my partner's lip off."
- "These aren't my lips."
- "My parents are watching."
- "It's amazing how I can still taste the anchovy pizza I had for breakfast."

What to Do

- Give yourself a nose bleed.
- Clear your throat.
- Blow a chewing-gum bubble.
- Flip your retainer in and out.
- Put pepperoni in your teeth.
- Let your dog out and give it a big slobbery kiss.

◆

*Adapted from *Creative Dating* by Doug Fields and Todd Temple (Nashville: Oliver-Nelson, 1986).

76. How do you get a member of the opposite sex to notice you?

We'll use the male species for the example since young women have more sense than to try anything suggested here.

When you see her, pretend that you are choking and hope that she has taken a CPR class. If she has and performs the Heimlich maneuver, you'll receive a few bruised ribs, but it will be worth it. Pretend to cough out the object—a bubble-gum projectile will be most convincing. Now tell her that she saved your life.

Explain to her that your life is now hers and you must follow her until you have an opportunity to return the favor. (She's probably seen *Robin Hood* so she knows how this works.)

Now follow her around everywhere she goes but hope she doesn't do anything too dangerous because you don't want to have to save her life so soon and risk not seeing her again.

Warning: If the P.E. coach comes to your rescue, you better hope he didn't see the movie.

◆

77. Who should you ask to the prom?

Ah…the prom: the magical evening when expectation is exceeded only by expense. Many students look forward to it for years. Some have contests to see how many they can attend, often cultivating friendships at different schools to get a higher score.

Asking someone that you don't know very well can lead to an uncomfortable and expensive evening. So if you're not dating someone but really want to go (so that in college you won't have to say, "No!" when someone asks if you went), ask a great friend to go with you. There won't be any of those lofty romantic expectations that can't possibly be fulfilled.

Instead, you can make a pact to have the most fun of any couple there.

Whether you go with the love of your life, your greatest friend, or your neighbor's niece, expect to have some good food and to dance your brains out. The popular thing may be to stay for dinner and one obligatory dance. But the fun is at the prom: the music and the people and the look on their faces when you show them the dance steps you've worked on for three weeks on the kitchen floor despite the snickers of your little sister and her two dozen best friends who watched you through the window.

DEATH

78. What happens to your body when you die?
79. What is a soul?
80. What happens to the soul when you die?
81. Where is heaven?
82. What is hell?
83. When people commit suicide, do they go to hell?
84. Are there any warning signs for suicide?
85. What should you do if you feel like committing suicide?
86. What do you say to someone who's lost a loved one?
87. What would happen to you if both your parents died?
88. What happens to your Social Security number when you die?

78. What happens to your body when you die?

Generally, when you die, your body is taken to a mortuary where it's prepared for burial or cremation. That usually means embalming, which includes replacing your blood with a fluid that preserves you during the few days between death and burial. Although embalming is not required for either burial or cremation, it is recommended if there is going to be any kind of viewing or visitation.

When a body is cremated, it is placed in a cardboard receptacle and put in the crematory, where the extremely hot temperatures transform the body into ashes. The ashes are then placed in another box or in an urn provided by the family.

◆

79. What is a soul?

Most people, regardless of their religion, believe that a person's essence exists in a soul that lives on after the body dies. The soul is a nonmaterial entity, so it doesn't show up in X rays and autopsies. Nor can it be destroyed by physical things.

◆

80. What happens to the soul when you die?

The Bible talks about people who die and instantly show up in front of God. If the body is still in the grave, something of themselves must make the journey. That's the soul.

What happens after this interview with God is a source of debate among theologians. Some say that the soul enters into heaven or hell immediately after God's judgment. Some say that a loving God would not condemn anyone to hell. Of course, no one, including these scholars, has had first-hand experience in the matter this side of death.

◆

81. Where is heaven?

Heaven is either (*a*) so far away that we can't spot it with a telescope or (*b*) hidden in another dimension. Or maybe we just have the perspective wrong. Heaven could be a big castle, and our entire universe could be a terrarium sitting on a table in a library in that castle.

We're pretty free to speculate on this stuff because the Bible doesn't have photos of heaven or maps showing where it is (is it right or left at the Big Dipper?).

◆

82. What is hell?

The Bible talks about hell as a fiery place where those who rebel against God end up spending eternity. It's a place of constant pain and suffering.

◆

83. When people commit suicide, do they go to hell?

If you use the Bible for your definition of hell, then you should use it to learn who goes there. The list of those who end up in hell includes all sorts of people who turn against God. But nowhere does it mention suicide victims.

◆

84. Are there any warning signs for suicide?

In his book *Why Suicide?*, Jerry Johnston outlines eleven deadly giveaways:[1]

1. Withdrawal
2. Moodiness
3. Depression
4. Aggression
5. Alcohol and drug abuse
6. Sexual activity
7. Eating disorders
8. Giving of prized possessions
9. Trauma
10. Personality change
11. Threat to do it

◆

85. What should you do if you feel like committing suicide?

Just about everyone experiences a fleeting moment when you wonder what it would be like to end it all. But if it is a preoccupation—something that has entered your mind more than once and more than fleetingly—it's time to tell someone.

Even if you feel that you have no friends or family who care, a legion of adults at churches, crisis centers, schools, and other places are committed to saving you—*just you*. Please don't become a statistic. Make a choice to contact one of these people before making any other choices. Here's how:

1. Check the phone book for the suicide hotline in your area. This call will be confidential. Someone will be

there to listen seven days a week, twenty-four hours a day. You have nothing to lose by making the call.

2. Talk to a friend or trusted adult (youth worker, teacher, parent, or counselor). Make the person aware of your thoughts or plans.

3. If you have designed a method, ask a friend or trusted adult to help you remove the instruments needed to proceed.

4. Make a contract with a friend or adult stating that you will contact that person before doing anything irreversible.

5. Avoid alcohol or drugs, which increase depression and get in the way of wise decision making.

6. Pray. Here's an ancient and powerful prayer first cried out to God by King David nearly three thousand years ago:

> Hear my cry, O God;
>   listen to my prayer.
> From the ends of the earth I call to you,
>   I call as my heart grows faint;
>   lead me to the rock that is higher than I.
>   (Psalm 61:1–2)

◆

86. What do you say to someone who's lost a loved one?

You want to say something that will take away the hurt. The truth is, *nothing* you say can take away the pain. Which is a good thing, because a person is *supposed* to feel pain when a loved one dies. It's part of what being human is all about.

Usually the best thing you can say is ... nothing. Just give a big hug to let the person know you care. The worst thing to do is to try to explain the reason for the person's death. If the grieving person has great acting skills, she will smile and nod, hoping that *you* are somehow comforted by your explanation. If you absolutely have to say something, tell the person you're sorry for her loss. If you knew the deceased, you can say you miss him.

---

87. What would happen to you if both your parents died?

Your parents likely have made arrangements for this occurrence, typically in their wills. You may want to ask them if they've made any plans. If your parents have made no arrangements, you'll become a ward of the court, and the judge will talk to your relatives to figure out who would make the best guardian. It's usually an aunt, uncle, or grandparent. Sometimes the judge will give custody to a close family friend. If no one steps forward to ask for custody, you'll remain in the care of the court, living in a group home or an individual foster home.

---

88. What happens to your Social Security number when you die?

It dies with you. Your number is uniquely yours. If the government chose to use every possible combination of the nine-digit number, it would have to assign a billion numbers before running out.

——DIVORCE——

89. How do you know if you caused your parents' divorce?
90. Do you have to obey a stepparent?
91. How do you get along with stepbrothers and stepsisters?
92. Can you turn out normal without having a father?
93. How do you deal with the emotions stirred up by your parents' divorce?
94. Who decides which parent you live with?
95. Your parents are divorced. As an adult, are you more likely to get a divorce?

89. How do you know if you caused your parents' divorce?

Guilt runs rampant in a family going through a divorce. *Someone* has to take the blame for the breakup. Most kids seem willing to point the finger at themselves. Young children especially feel the need to claim the blame. One study showed that almost 75 percent of six-year-olds of divorce believed they were the cause of their parents' split.[1] Older kids aren't as harsh on themselves, but they still feel guilt.

This information may deflate your ego a bit, but divorce is one piece of mischief you can't cause. Here are the facts:

- Childless couples get divorced for the same reasons your parents did; children weren't the cause of their breakups. Neither were they the cause of your parents' divorce.

- Many couples in trouble have children as a way of resolving the problems; the children blame themselves for a problem that began before they were born.

- Some of your parents' problems were rooted in *their* childhoods, not yours.

- Parents stay together *for the sake of* their kids; your parents' problems were so great that not even this could keep them together.

Unfortunately, the facts can't take away the hurt and the anger. The only thing that can is forgiveness. That means forgiving your parents for what they've done to your life, forgiving yourself for the part you think you played in it. This isn't an easy thing. It can take years. Some people never forgive. You can tell who they are because the hurt and anger work like poison in their friendships and in their marriages.

If you're struggling with these feelings, talk to a friend who's going through it, too. Together you can admit your pain and take the first step toward forgiveness.

◆

90. Do you have to obey a stepparent?

Legally No. There's no law that says you must obey a stepparent, unless that person is also your legal guardian.

Morally Yes. While you're living at home, you should obey the heads of that home. Disobeying a stepparent causes all sorts of problems.

1. It hurts your parent because you're showing disrespect for someone he or she loves.
2. It creates tension between the two of them because your parent has to step into the middle.
3. It turns your parent against you because he or she will feel obligated to side with the underdog, which is the "new" member of the family.
4. It creates more tension between your parents because one of them will assume that your disobedience is a way of acting out your anger over the divorce.
5. It makes life tougher for your younger brothers and sisters who may have to bear the wrath of an angry stepparent (they also have to live with a bad situation after you move out).
6. If the stepparent has kids, they'll see how you treat *their* parent and treat *your* parent the same way.

In other words, it's not worth it. If you have problems with obeying a stepparent, get the three of you to sit down and agree together on the rules and consequences.

◆

91. How do you get along with stepbrothers and stepsisters?

The Brady Bunch made it look so easy. Mom and Dad get married, and suddenly it's one big happy family. The only serious conflict was between the dog and the cat—and the cat got dropped from the show.

In the real world, blended families are a lot of work. When you're an adult, you discover how hard it is to find someone you get along with so well that you can stand living under the same roof. The odds of all the kids feeling the same way from the start are pretty slim.

The good news is that, over time, stepbrothers and stepsisters usually enjoy living in the same house and sometimes become best friends. These tips will help you get there:

Cut your folks some slack. If the marriage was recent, they may still be trying hard—maybe a bit *too* hard—to get you to be brothers and sisters. They'll lighten up after a while. They'll do so more quickly if they sense that you're willing to give it your best shot.

Be friends first. It's a lot to ask to go from strangers to siblings in a short time. Work on the friendship part first.

Be a big brother. Or sister. More kids mean more competition for attention. Spend extra time with the younger ones so they don't feel left out.

Respect their parent. No one likes to see his parent treated badly. Your stepsiblings will get along with you a lot better if you try to get along with their parent. (They'll also treat *your* parent with more respect.)

———————◆———————

92. Can you turn out normal without having a father?

Yes, but it's harder. Studies consistently show that children who have two healthy parents adjust better to life's situations. But you aren't doomed to abnormality. You can make up for much of what's missing. Seek out someone who can fill parts of that role. A youth pastor, an uncle, or a grandparent can supply some of the wisdom of years that all of us need.

———————◆———————

93. How do you deal with the emotions stirred up by your parents' divorce?

Divorce stirs up a whirlwind of emotions: guilt, anger, hatred, hurt, remorse, shame, rejection. Some of these feelings can swirl around inside you for years and years after your parents' divorce. Here's what you can do about these feelings:

- Keep them inside and pretend that everything's okay. Wait about fifteen years and then take them out on your children. Surprise!
- Go berserk—get drunk, sleep around, steal stuff. When people ask why, tell them you're just "acting out."
- Talk to someone. Describe your feelings. Ask for help in dealing with them. Then start to work on forgiveness (see question 89).

◆

94. Who decides which parent you live with?

If your parents can't reach an agreement on their own, the court will step in to decide on the custody arrangement. Family law varies from state to state, but kids under twelve generally don't get to pick (although your preference is considered). After that age your opinion bears more weight. In California, for example, the law requires that you be asked who you prefer to live with. That doesn't mean you'll get your wish. As long as you're a minor living at home, the court has the right to make the decision based on what the court thinks is best.

If the custody issue becomes a battle between your parents, one of them will eventually "win." That puts you in an uncomfortable position with the loser. It's a bad situation, but it's *not* your fault. Fortunately, you can make it a bit better. As much as you're capable of, affirm your love to the losing parent, who can't help feeling that he or she has lost you. Make the most of your visits, and use the telephone to stay in touch.

————————— ◆ —————————

95. Your parents are divorced. As an adult, are you more likely to get a divorce?

Studies of the effects on children of divorce have shown that this is true. One University of Texas study found that white women who were younger than sixteen when their parents were divorced were 59 percent more likely to become divorced or separated. White men were 32 percent more likely. Black men and women were 15 to 16 percent more likely.

The people who did the best in the study were ones whose folks continued to share in parenting decisions and were able to communicate civilly.[2]

So if your parents went through an ugly divorce, does that mean your marriage will be doomed to fail, too? Of course not. Since you now know that some stuff in your past could somehow cause trouble for you later on, you can work to prevent that from happening (knowledge is power). Lots of couples go through premarital counseling to work through potential problems before they get a chance to do damage. That's a good idea whether your parents are together or not.

——FAMILY——

96. How can you show parents that you love them?
97. What do you do if a family member is abusing you?
98. If living at home becomes impossible, what are your options?
99. What happens if you run away?
100. You're adopted and would like to meet your biological mother. What do you do?
101. How do you know when it's time to move out?
102. What are the best and the worst parts about moving out?
103. Is it wrong to live at home after you're an adult?
104. How do you tell your grandparents you love them?
105. How do you make your grandparents feel more a part of family gatherings?
106. What are some good gifts for grandparents and other older relatives?

96. How can you show parents that you love them?

Parents can be as insecure about your feelings for them as you can be about their feelings for you. Everyone needs frequent reassurance. Here's how you can express your love creatively:

- Pick flowers from your neighbors' yards (ask first), and give a great big bouquet.
- Hide a note in a briefcase, purse, or pocket that will be discovered later.
- Support a sport or hobby: hide golf balls in his coat pockets, protein bars in her gym bag.
- Detail the car.
- Take them to breakfast on Saturday morning.
- Make a booklet of coupons redeemable for back rubs, household chores, yard work, and breakfast in bed.
- Clean your room or make dinner without being asked.
- Listen to their stories about the past—childhood, family history, school, dating.
- Throw a "Just Because" surprise party with family and friends.
- Make some new refrigerator art. They miss those strange scribblings you used to bring home from grade school.
- Mail greeting cards to them at work and at home. Send them for big and small occasions, including birthdays, anniversaries, Arbor Day, and Groundhog Day.
- Just say, "I love you."

◆

97. What do you do if a family member is abusing you?

Tell someone now!

That's probably not the answer you wanted, but it's the only one that works. The person who is abusing you is sick and needs help now. There can be no behavior on your part that warrants abuse. No matter what you do, no one is allowed to harm you physically, sexually, emotionally, or psychologically.

Whom do you tell? You have several choices.

- *Child Abuse Hotline.* There is one in every city, and the number can be found by looking in any phone book or by calling information. It is a confidential line.
- *Police.* Most police departments have someone specially trained to handle such situations.
- *Trusted teacher, youth minister, or counselor.* She has the legal responsibility to report all cases of abuse. She will know who to contact and will be able to help you figure out what to do.
- *Parent of a friend.* If you can't talk to a professional, at least talk to someone who cares for you. Another parent may be able to comfort you but may not know how to remedy the situation.

———————— ◆ ————————

98. If living at home becomes impossible, what are your options?

Get Someone to Intervene Ask a youth worker or counselor to act as referee between you and your parents while you discuss the problems and solutions.

Call for Help If the problem is abuse, contact the police, a teacher, youth minister, counselor, or abuse hotline. You will get help to decide what to do next.

Stay with Others Ask if you may stay temporarily with friends or relatives till things cool down.

Emancipate Begin the process of emancipation, which allows you to move out on your own before age eighteen (see question 157).

Run to a Friend If you must run, run to a friend.

———————— ◆ ————————

99. What happens if you run away?

Running away is against the law. If the police find you at any time, they can take you into custody and call your parents to come and get you. The consequences of not getting caught are worse. Most teenagers who run away and stay away end up living on the streets because landlords don't rent to minors. Employers don't hire them because they have no address or phone number. Many runaways make money by stealing, dealing drugs, or becoming prostitutes.

Almost no one runs from a good situation. If you run because of abuse and are picked up by the police, they will not take you home if you tell them your reasons for running. Instead, they'll take you to a youth shelter.

If life at home ever becomes life-threatening and you have to run away, run to a friend's house instead of the street.

———————— ◆ ————————

100. You're adopted and would like to meet your biological mother. What do you do?

First, search your reasons for wanting to meet her. For some, it's to find out about hereditary traits and diseases, life expectancy, family history and culture. For others, it's a personal vendetta—a need to interrogate the woman and discover why she gave you up (or, even worse, as a way to hurt your adoptive folks). For many, it's just extreme curiosity.

Second, prepare yourself for the best and the worst. Seeking your biological mother can be very positive for both of you. It can be a healing experience: you resolve a sense of abandonment, and she sees the product of her creation. But it can also be a nightmare: she might have been a rape victim; she might have had psychological problems; she might have a family of her own, and *they* might not know of her pregnancy long ago.

Third, have some long talks with your parents. If they're strongly opposed, they may be trying to protect you from one of these nightmares.

If you decide to seek your biological mother, your search will depend on the form of the adoption. In a *closed* adoption, the identity of the biological mother is never revealed to your parents, so you're on your own to discover her. In an *open* adoption, the biological mother can interview prospective parents, so your folks would know who she is.

If you were separated from your biological mother by a government agency that decided she was unable or unfit to care for you, your adoptive parents would probably know all about your original parents.

Regardless of whether you seek your biological parents, make sure you communicate your love to your adoptive ones. Most of us realize that, in a sense, our parents *have to* love us—they took what they got. But *your* parents *chose* to love you—they took exactly what they wanted.

———————— ◆ ————————

101. How do you know when it's time to move out?

This is a tough decision, but sometimes parents will give pretty good clues. You know it's time to move out if...

...You come home from a week at summer camp and discover your parents have moved and left no forwarding address.

...You come home from school to find everything you own sitting on the front porch.

...You find an eviction notice posted to your bedroom door.

...Your folks rent out your bedroom during school hours to a person who works nights.

...Your dog brings you the morning paper—already opened to the "room for rent" section of the classifieds.

◆

102. What are the best and the worst parts about moving out?

Best

- You can stay up all night and eat an entire chocolate cake *in bed*.
- You can wear whatever you want for as many days in a row as you want.
- Your relationship with your parents usually begins to improve because the time you spend together is more special, less connected with discipline issues.
- Life suddenly looks different. You get new dreams and develop new interests. You appreciate things more.

Worst

- After a few nights of staying up all night and eating chocolate cake in bed, you develop black eyes, chubby thighs, a wobbly walk, and a tendency to drool.
- You discover that clothes are *outrageously* expensive, get dirty and wrinkled *way* too fast, and *eat* time and money to launder, fold, and iron every week. (Getting socks and underwear for Christmas used to be a disappointment—now they're your favorite gifts.)
- The *best* roommates can be complete jerks at times; the

worst roommates push you to the edge of sanity. (Every family has a different way of doing things: roommate situations are, in effect, cross-cultural experiences.)

- Everything costs money. Most people spend their time either working themselves into debt or trying to drag themselves out of it.
- Let's be honest here. It's scary and very lonely sometimes.

———————— ◆ ————————

103. Is it wrong to live at home after you're an adult?

No. More than half of eighteen- to twenty-four-year-olds live with their parents.[1] Some have never left; others have returned after a stint on their own. Once upon a time people got married so young that they almost always moved from their parents' nest to their own on their wedding day. People postpone marriage longer nowadays so they stay at home longer.

The best advantage of living at home is financial. It's easier to save money for school, a business, or a house if you have little or no monthly rent.

———————— ◆ ————————

104. How do you tell your grandparents you love them?

Here are a few creative love messages:

- Send a love letter. Write a simple letter telling her all the things you love about her. Chances are, the last time you did that you were five years old (and she probably kept it).

- Embroider an I Love You pillowcase. It only takes twenty-three big stitches.
- Shoot an I Love You video. Interview family members and have them say what they appreciate about Grandma. Show gifts and other mementos that remind them of her; describe their favorite times together. Mail the video, or show it at a family gathering.
- Donate money to the American Heart Association in their names.
- Just say it. It's a quick call. (How about right now?)

◆

105. How do you make your grand-parents feel more a part of family gatherings?

Busy lives and smaller and more spread-out families keep many of us from connecting with our own heritage. Your best link is your grandparents. Go out of your way to include them in your family's activities. Here are a few ideas to help you connect the generations:

Hand-Me-Down Cooking Cookbooks are a new invention. Before they showed up, people learned all their recipes from family and friends, passing them from generation to generation. Make sure the process doesn't stop in your family. Prepare and serve an old family recipe with your grandparent acting as master chef and you playing the protégé.

Traditions Traditions bind a family together when all else around them is changing. Ask your grandparent to help you re-create some holiday traditions he remembers from his childhood. Make them a regular part of future holidays at your house, and pass them on to your kids.

Namesakes At a family gathering ask your grandmother to tell everyone who her parents were named after, how her own name was chosen, and how she chose the names of her children (your parent, aunts, and uncles). Pass the baton to your parents, and find out why they chose the names of you and your siblings. Finally, talk about the names you'd like to give your kids.

Storytime Ask your grandparent to tell a story he remembers hearing from his parents or grandparents. Memorize the story and retell it to him at the next gathering to make sure you got it straight. You'll need to know it so you can tell your own kids.

Three-Story Views Ask a question and let each generation answer it. For example, ask everyone to describe what elementary school was like. Gramps gets another opportunity to embellish the distance and the depth of the snow he trudged through on his way to school. Your mom can talk about how girls were sent home from school for wearing pants. You can describe the computers you programmed in your kindergarten class.

Childhood Visit If possible, take a family trip to the place where your grandfather grew up. A walk down memory lane will be fun for him, and it will give you a sense of your own heritage.

For even more ideas on how to treat older folks, check out *52 Simple Ways to Show Aging Parents You Care* by Tracy Green and Todd Temple (Nashville: Oliver-Nelson, 1992).

———————— ◆ ————————

106. What are some good gifts for grandparents and other older relatives?

You don't have to spend a lot to give them gifts they'll love to get:

- *Saturday servant certificate.* Design a certificate stating that you'll give a whole Saturday for helping with household chores, cleaning, painting, yard work, or whatever.

- *Flowers.* Put some red geraniums or an indoor plant in a nice flowerpot, or prepare an herb garden.

- *Top-five list.* Have everybody in the family list five favorite memories with Grandma. Make it into a booklet, and put the family picture on the cover.

- *Birthday board.* Paint all the dates of family birthdays in bright colors on a wooden cutting board to be hung on the wall.

- *Freeze time.* Find a picture of your grandfather at about six years old, your father at about the same age, and you about the same age. Have them framed together.

- *Give it back.* Wrap up your granddad's old fishing pole and give it back to him with an invitation to join you for a picnic at the lake.

- *Easy phone.* Get your siblings to pitch in and buy your grandparents a phone with big number keys and speed dial. Show them how to program the numbers into memory.

——— FRIENDS ———

107. How do you find friends?

When it comes to making friends, dogs have it made. Take a golden retriever. The moment he spots another canine, a silly grin comes over his face. His body quivers uncontrollably. He begins to slobber. The tail goes ballistic. If the other dog reacts the same way, they meet, sniff, and romp. Now they're friends.

We humans don't behave that way (if you *do*, you'll be hauled off to the people pound). A retriever sees every dog as a potential friend—even a schnauzer. Imagine if we approached friendship the same way: every person is a potential friend—even one who looks like a schnauzer.

We exclude a lot of people who would make great friends. We write them off because of the way they look, the crowd they hang out with, the clothes they wear, how much money they have, the music they listen to, the color of their skin—all the wrong reasons.

If you want to make new friends, remove these self-imposed restrictions and just talk to people. Here's where:

- *In class.* Ask the person next to you a question about the lesson or notes from yesterday or help with a project—anything to break the ice. People like to be helpful. (This isn't such a good idea during tests.)

- *In a group.* Join a club, sports league, or church youth group—any group where you'll meet new people.

- *At work.* Working with someone is just about the easiest way to get acquainted because it happens automatically.

- *On a project.* Volunteer to help on a fund-raising project, blood drive, food collection, whatever.

- *In public.* Be friendly to people you run into throughout the day: store clerks, busboys, the person who takes your order at a restaurant, the girl in line with you at the post office. Maybe, just maybe, you'll find something to talk about and become best friends or get married or something. But you'll never know if you just stay on your leash.

◆

108. How do you keep a friendship going strong?

First, you have to figure out what the perfect friend would be like. Here's a wild guess:

- Someone who listens to your stories, even the stupid ones
- Someone who laughs at your jokes, including the ones that no one else finds funny
- Someone who calls you for no reason except to see how you're doing
- Someone you could tell your deepest, darkest secret to and know that (*a*) he'd still be your friend and (*b*) he'd keep it a secret
- Someone who sticks up for you when other people put you down, whether it's in your presence or behind your back
- Someone you could ask to help you with all your chores and know she'd do it
- Someone who tells you you're good-looking and smart and funny and talented
- Someone who'd trust you with her deepest, darkest secrets
- Someone who cares enough to tell you when you're messing up
- Someone who tells you when he's angry with you instead of making you figure it out

You probably can think of other qualities. Once you know what the perfect friend would be like, the next step is to *become* that kind of friend.

Try this experiment. Write "I am" in front of the qualities listed. Now think of your best friend and rank how well you do on each of the statements, using *never, seldom, sometimes, usually,* and *always.* For example, "I am someone who sticks up for Mark when other people put him down." *Al-*

ways? Sometimes? Do the same self-evaluation on other friendships and see how you rate.

The next step is the easiest...and the hardest. Pick your weakest areas and go to work. What's going to have to change before you'll be able to answer *always* to every statement?

The process of getting there is exactly how you keep a friendship going strong.

◆

109. Is it ever right to betray a friend's secret?

Ninety-five times out of a hundred it would not be right to share a friend's secret. What's *told* in confidence is supposed to be *kept* in confidence. So, what about the other five times? If your friend is in a potentially harmful situation (abuse, suicide, drugs, alcohol in the family), you may need to break one commitment to keep a greater one: your friend's safety.

If your friend's life or health is being threatened, tell someone. That someone must be a person who can be completely trusted to act in the best interests of your friend—not someone who will want information for malicious intent. Counselors and youth leaders make great sounding boards. They can help you figure out what to do next.

◆

110. What do you do if a friend is really messing up in life?

The real test of a friendship is what happens when one friend blows it. What you do in response determines the kind of friend you are. If your friend is abusing alcohol, using drugs, ruining his health, breaking the law, or making stupid sexual or moral choices, here's what you can do:

- *Get the facts.* In a court of law a person is innocent until proven guilty. Give your friend the same presumption of innocence. Find out if there's really a problem. Ask questions.

- *Get involved.* A friendship is a commitment. If there *is* a problem, you have the right and responsibility to do something about it (although your friend will probably disagree). Now more than ever he needs a caring friend with a level head. Make yourself more available and more interested than ever.

- *Act out of love.* When you're messing up, it's easy to think that anyone who asks you what's going on is just looking for evidence to bust you. That's what your friend is thinking now. You'll have to go overboard to prove that you really do care: "I care about you, and there's nothing you can do to change that."

- *Call for help.* If your friend is in way over his head, forget about playing junior psychologist. There's too much at stake. Talk to a trusted adult—a counselor, teacher, youth worker, minister. He or she can advise you on what to do next.

◆

111. What can you do when a friend is in a crisis?

Personal crisis comes in many forms:

- Parents splitting up
- Violence in the home
- Alcohol in the family
- Drug addiction

- Rape
- Death of a loved one
- Serious injury
- Disease
- Severe depression
- Pregnancy
- End of a relationship
- Suicide attempt
- Trouble with the law

Whatever the trauma, the person best situated to help him get through it is you. People who make it through a crisis cite friends as one key to their recovery. Here's what a friend in crisis needs from you most:

Your presence. Crisis is scary. Drop what you're doing and be there.

Your ear. Don't try to say all the right things and solve all his problems. Just listen.

Your encouragement. Most crises put people into depression. Let him know how much he means to you. Call him frequently; take him gifts; let him laugh.

Your prayers. God is a pro at planting seeds of hope in people's hearts. Ask Him to go to work on your friend. Then tell your friend what you've been talking to God about.

Your wisdom. People do incredibly foolish things in a crisis. Sometimes their *reaction* to a crisis is worse than the crisis itself (suicide, for example). Be there to provide wisdom and common sense—help him think through his decisions.

Sometimes it takes a crisis to get a person to deal with a problem such as alcoholism or family violence. Now is the best time for him to deal with it. Do not let the crisis pass without seeking professional help. If your friend is unwilling or unable to make the phone call, do it for him.

──FUN──

112. How do you learn to snowboard?

Snowboarding is *kind of* like a few other sports, including surfing, skiing, and skateboarding. But skill in any or all of these sports doesn't automatically make you a snowboarder.

For one thing, snowboarding is just about the only sport where your feet are strapped together. This fact becomes obvious the first time you strap in. You feel yourself starting to fall so you put one foot out to stop you. It won't move. Down you go. Without the free use of your feet, your rear and wrists take a beating. Wrist injuries are so common in snowboarding that you're foolish to try to learn without wrist braces.

A snowboard with boots rents for about $30 a day. Snowboard rentals are harder to find than skis; shops that rent them usually have a limited inventory, so it's best to reserve your equipment a week or two in advance. If you get hooked and decide to buy, expect to pay between $250 and $700 for a board and bindings. Most snowboarders use standard snowboots rather than custom snowboard boots: a good pair of snowboots costs $100 to $150.

The best place to start learning is on a bunny slope with a patient snowboarder friend. She can show you the simple yet essential steps involved in turning. When you've mastered them in slow motion, you can move to steeper slopes.

◆

113. How do you learn windsurfing?

Windsurfing requires just two natural ingredients: wind and water (a light breeze of the former, about three feet deep of the latter). And it just so happens that these two ingredients can be found almost anywhere in the United States. No matter where you live, you're probably not too far from an ocean, bay, lake, river, pond, or puddle. Oh, and you'll need a sailboard.

Which is just like a sail*boat*, except different. On a sailboat, you hold the sail in place with a sheet (a sailor's way of saying "rope") connected to the boom (pole used to hold the sail open and to smack you in the head whenever it feels like it). Sailboarders keep the sail in place by holding the boom with their hands. It's less likely to bonk you on the head that way, but your arms feel the effects.

Another missing part: the rudder. You steer by changing the angles of the sail. A universal joint where the mast attaches to the board permits the mast-boom-sail combination to move to any angle you choose. These differences create a vehicle that can skim the surface at 20 mph, carve a white arc in a wave face, or launch you off a swell and into the sky.

Basic windsurfing isn't difficult to learn: two to four hours with a good instructor and a light breeze will get you sailing on your own. A beginner's lesson will run you about $50 to $70 including the board. If you have a friend with a good beginner's board, you may be able to learn for free.

If you fall in love with the sport, you'll start running up a tab. Board rentals run about $45 a day for a basic rig, $60 for a nice setup. And buying a basic board with all the trimmings will cost about $500. If you have to buy a red Range Rover to carry the board to the water, add another $46,000.

———————— ◆ ————————

114. How do you learn hang gliding?

Go ahead. Step to the edge of the cliff. Now jump off. That's how a hang glider starts his ride. Here's how it works.

A hang glider has a glide ratio of 10:1, which means that it flies ten feet forward for every one foot it falls. (Interesting fact: watermelons, cows, and Mazda Miatas have glide ratios of 0:1—they fly *zero* feet forward for every foot they drop.)

The typical hang glider has a sink rate of two hundred feet per minute. That is, if you jumped off a two-hundred-foot cliff—and held onto the glider—you'd touch the ground one minute later. (For comparison, if you jumped off that cliff in a kitchen sink, you'd touch down in less than three seconds; the sink's sink rate: thirty-two feet per second.)

But hang glider pilots are like the rest of us: they want the good times to last. So they manage to stay in the air longer by flying in *lifts*. Thermal lifts are columns of warm air that rise through cooler air, sometimes for thousands of feet. Glider pilots stay inside these ascending columns by circling—like flying a circular staircase. A bird soaring upward in a steady circle is a sign of a thermal lift (or it could just be circling a dead hang glider). Ridge lifts are formed when the wind blows into the steep face of a hill, cliff, or building. The air must escape somewhere, so it spills upward and over the ridge. Hang gliders can fly these ridges as long as they stay near the edge—sometimes for miles in one direction.

Hang gliding is real flying, and learning to fly requires study. A beginner's course includes several hours of ground school (maybe even *homework*), a tandem flight with the instructor, six to eight hours of practice on a small training hill, and your first solo flight. The course may run three days and costs about $225. (If you just want to try hang gliding for the experience, you can take a tandem ride with a pro for about $75.)

If you discover that hang gliding is your thing, you better have a good source of cash. Going beyond the beginner level can run you several hundred dollars in lessons and many days of glider rentals at $40 per day. If you buy your own outfit, you'll need about $3,000. And if your mother ever sees you flying, you may have to pay for her heart attack.

———————— ◆ ————————

115. How do you learn scuba diving?

The first time you scuba dive you feel like you're breaking the rules. All your life you've been taught to hold your breath while underwater: if you try to inhale, you drown. Then along comes your scuba instructor, who tells you that holding your breath while rising to the surface is wrong, bad, naughty—and can kill you.

Then there's the rule about never going deeper than twelve feet, which you made up yourself that time you swam to the bottom of the big pool. Your ears started to hurt, your lungs were chanting, WE WANT AIR! WE WANT AIR! and your brain was commanding you to return to the surface immediately or risk being sucked down the drain. Now you're swimming forty feet beneath the ocean's surface, and you're *still alive*. You can't help feeling your dad will send you to your room when he finds out how disobedient you've been.

But you're not really breaking the rules. You're learning a whole new set designed to make diving safer. The scuba certification course is about forty hours, usually spread over two or three weekends. In addition to pool and ocean (or lake) dives, you'll spend time in the classroom learning about air and water pressure and why your ears and lungs will explode if you don't learn your lessons. Since scuba diving takes you into another world, your instructor will also teach you the customs of the natives (sharks and eels and stuff).

The cost of a dive course is about $200, and the instructor provides the equipment. Some courses have an age minimum of fourteen; others are open to people as young as twelve. If you're under fourteen, you may have to call around a bit to find a course that will accept you.

Assuming you have your own mask, fins, and snorkel, you can rent scuba equipment for $35 per day (you must show your diver's certification card to rent or buy dive gear). If you want to buy your own bare-bones outfit, you'll leave the store $500 lighter. Add $1.5 million for a nice 150-foot dive yacht.

◆

116. How do you learn to surf?

The three things you need to learn to surf are the right board, the right waves, and the right stand.

Board The easiest for learning is an egg-shaped board (blunt nose and tail) about two feet longer than your body. It floats well so it's easier to paddle and stand on, and the blunt nose gives it stability and keeps above the water better (beginners tend to drive narrow boards straight underwater at the bottom of a wave). The wrong board can make learning difficult, if not impossible.

Don't spend a lot of money on a board until after you learn. Boards come in lots of shapes and styles, and you won't know what's best for you until you've surfed for a while. A new board can run $250 or more. You can pick up a decent used board from a surf shop for $50 to $150 depending on how thrashed it is. You look pretty silly when you first start surfing—no matter how good your board looks.

Waves The best learning waves break slowly and gently, giving you time to get into position and stand up. Fast, steep waves are very unforgiving. If you hesitate, you're gone.

Stand Most people fall as they're trying to get up. Practice getting up by laying the board on soft sand (dig a hole for the fins). Getting up is done in one smooth, quick move. When the wave catches the board, stop paddling, and grip the board by the rails (sides) near your chest; do a push-up but drag your feet up under your body, then stand and let go of the rails. Have someone show you the move a few times, including where your feet should be when you're done. Once you've got it wired, you're ready to get wet.

———————— ◆ ————————

117. What's bodysurfing?

It's the most natural form of surfing: it's just you, the wave, and your swimsuit. (And if your suit isn't tied tight, it becomes just you and the wave.) Swim fins can help you catch more waves and prevent your swimsuit from coming off completely. Basically, you wait until the wave is ready to break, then swim for shore until the wave catches you.

The trick to all surfing—especially bodysurfing—is timing.

If you start swimming too early, the wave breaks behind you. If you're just a little early, it breaks *on* you. If you take off too late, the wave passes you by. And if you're just a little late on a big wave, you may get launched from the top of it, risking a broken neck if you hit the bottom when you land.

The best way to learn bodysurfing is to spend ten minutes with someone who knows how. He can show you when and where to take off—and how to bail out safely.

◆

118. What's bodyboarding?

Bodyboarding is surfing lying down. It's been around a long time. Before Morey Boogies and other "sponge" boards came along, people bodyboarded on sheets of plywood, rubber rafts, and stubby little surfboards called bellyboards.

Bodyboarding on a sponge board is the safest and easiest kind of surfing to learn. You just line yourself up where the waves are about to break, kick like crazy till the wave catches you, then let it take you away. Swim fins aren't essential, but you'll probably catch twice as many waves if you wear them.

The cheapest bodyboard will cost you $30 to $50 and will deliver plenty of fun for the money. Top-of-the-line models can run up to $200. A good pair of surf fins (Duck Feet, Churchill, Viper) costs about $40.

◆

119. What's there to do on a Friday night?

Friday night: The night half the people sit at home wishing they were having as much fun as the other half are pretending to have.

If you and your friends are tired of sitting *and* pretending, here are some fun and strange things you can do:

- *Iceblocking.* It's a great activity for warm nights. Take a block of ice to the top of a steep grassy hill. Sit on the block (a towel keeps numbing to a minimum). Lift your feet. Scream all the way down. If you and your block survive, do it all again.

- *Spanish film.* Find a theater that plays Spanish-language films. Watch a movie. After the film, go out for a Coke and try to figure out what happened in the film (you'll be surprised at how much you understand and enjoy).

- *Air show.* Build paper airplanes and fly them from the roof or upstairs window. Hold contests for speed, distance, freestyle flying, strangest-looking craft.

- *Food lab.* Now's the time to test and taste that strange recipe you've been thinking about—the broccoli tops dipped in chocolate or the baked pineapple stuffed with Skippy (the peanut butter, not the dog).

- *Bowling.* Sure, it's no big deal if you go bowling *every* Friday night...but if you haven't been bowling since your tenth birthday party, you're going to have a lot of fun.

- *Treasure hunt.* Set up a complex treasure hunt on Friday afternoon, hiding clues in pay phone yellow pages, airport luggage lockers, public fountains, bookstore shelves, and under the counter at the Dairy Queen. Give your friends their first clue and track them through the hunt. Winner plans next week's hunt.

- *Free performance.* Somewhere in your area someone is performing for free. Check the activities calendar in the local paper for a listing of free concerts, plays, Russian dance performances, and Persian poetry readings.

——FUTURE——

120. How do you become a zookeeper?

A zookeeper is involved in all aspects of the care of animals. From scooping the poop to microwaving carrots for a finicky eater to conducting research on mating habits—the keeper does it all. In a larger zoo you usually get assigned to one species and often aren't given a choice about which one.

A love for animals and a desire to see them lead happy lives are essential. A college degree is not necessary, but it is helpful. You needn't major in one of the sciences, but a degree (or interest in obtaining a degree) in biology or zoology is beneficial. It shows that you have a real interest in the subject—something employers always look for.

If you're interested in zookeeping as a career, you may want to test it out with a summer job at the zoo—selling peanuts while working for them.

◆

121. What does it take to become a veterinarian?

A sense of adventure. While a medical doctor must learn only the workings of humans, vets must explore a plethora of species. An undergraduate degree in biology is not required but is definitely preferred. Then there are three years of veterinarian school.

Veterinary medicine is a popular field. There's lots of competition to get in, and only twenty-seven vet schools in the country enable you to get there. That means you have to have very good grades and a determination to make it.

◆

122. What does it take to become the president?

Based on past examples, you must be a white male with access to lots of money. Okay, the real requirements are that you must...

- be a natural-born citizen of the U.S.
- have lived in the U.S. for the past fourteen years.
- be age thirty-five or older.
- never have been convicted of a felony.

———————— ◆ ————————

123. What are your chances of making it as a recording star?

Record companies are not cultural foundations set up to enrich society. They're not artist guilds set up to give people an outlet for musical expression.

Record companies are businesses. Their primary goal: make money. If you can help them do that, they may want to do business with you.

Talent is important because most people prefer to buy albums by good musicians. When record company people listen to you, they're listening for something that will *sell*.

Timing helps, too. For example, when rap music first became popular, a lot of untalented musicians got record contracts. The public wanted rap music, and the record companies had to scramble to meet the demand. Now more rap artists are out there so the record companies can be more selective.

Your chances for success also depend on where you live. Artists and producers tend to congregate in certain cities. Los Angeles and New York are big for most kinds of music, especially rap and hip-hop. The country and gospel music capital is Nashville. Atlanta is becoming a popular place for both rock and country musicians.

The biggest factor is determination—your ability to continue producing music in the midst of continuous rejection and fickle music trends.

◆

124. What does it take to become a lawyer?

Most attorneys attend four years of college, then three years of law school. To practice law in a particular state, you must pass the state's bar exam—typically a three-day multipart test of knowledge, skill, and stamina. It is not necessary to study prelaw in undergraduate courses or even to obtain an undergraduate degree before attending law school. However, in most states it is necessary to go through some schooling before you are put through the grueling bar exam.

◆

125. How do you become a doctor?

If you hate to study and love to sleep in, choose another career: physicians go through more schooling than any other profession. To practice medicine, you have to attend medical school—typically a four-year stint.

To get into med school, you have to pass the MCAT, an exam that makes the SAT seem like a kindergarten quiz. If you make it into med school, you'll spend your years studying all aspects of medicine, practicing your new skills first on dead people, then on live ones.

After medical school come the "boards"—grueling tests that apply what you've learned and determine how well you've retained it. When you pass that milestone, people start calling you doctor. That's the good news.

The bad news is that you've got three or more years of residency ahead of you before they'll let you loose to practice medicine on your own.

———————————— ◆ ————————————

126. How do you become a circus clown?

There's a definite hierarchy in the clown world.

Clown Level 1   Amateur clowns are people who take up clowning as a hobby. They have little or no formal training. They clown around for family and friends and do free performances at schools, churches, and other groups.

Clown Level 2   These professional clowns work part time or full time performing at parties, festivals, and community events. Typically, they've attended clown classes through a local college or learned the art from another clown.

Clown Level 3   Traveling circus clowns are the cream of the clown crop. These pros go through lots of training. The Ringling Brothers and Barnum & Bailey Circus's clown college, for example, is a lot like a military boot camp, with vigorous physical conditioning and long hours of training and rehearsal. Only the best make it under the Big Top.

———————————— ◆ ————————————

127. What happens when you enlist in the military?

If you're thinking of joining the military to escape from your parents, you should know that the mother of all fathers exists in the form of your drill instructor. But if you're looking for technical training, discipline, adventure, and a sense of accomplishment, it's worth considering.

Each branch of the military has different criteria for entry, but all require a high-school diploma (some will accept a GED). The minimum age is seventeen or eighteen, depending on the branch. The maximum age for enlistment is twenty-seven for all branches but the army, which will take you if you're under thirty-five.

Before accepting you, the recruiter will determine if you're morally, mentally, and physically qualified. You'll have an interview with a recruiter, a mental aptitude test, and a series of physical and medical tests. If you pass these tests, you meet with a guidance counselor to determine what job you're best suited to train for. After that you head off to basic training.

Basic training introduces you to military life and prepares you for what you might encounter in combat. It lasts from two to three months. Those who go through it usually look back and say it was one of the toughest, most frightening, and most satisfying experiences of their lives.

After basic training comes job training. Depending on your job assignment, this process can take from two weeks to more than a year. When training is complete, you're assigned to a position somewhere in the world. You may be transferred to a new location or attend more schooling frequently throughout your stint. One of the excitements and difficulties of military life can be this constant shuffling from base to base.

Your commitment to the military may be as brief as two years (plus training time) or as long as six years, with the opportunity to reenlist if you've done a good job.

———————— ◆ ————————

128. What does it take to become a spy?

The U.S. government has two main agencies to take care of the sneaky stuff: the FBI and the CIA.

The FBI   The Federal Bureau of Investigation takes care of drug smugglers, fugitives, bank robbers, kidnappers, and other big-time criminals. To join the FBI, you must be a U.S. citizen between the ages of twenty-three and thirty-seven with a four-year college degree. You must have normal hearing, 20/20 vision (corrective lenses are okay), and no physical defects. You fill out an application, and if they like what they see, you'll be given a bunch of tests. These include a psychological test, a strenuous physical test, an examination by a panel of agents, and a fifteen-year background check. The whole process can take up to two years, and that's just to get in. You still have to go through the training program, which is extremely difficult.

The CIA   The Central Intelligence Agency gathers information that's essential in order to protect the United States. The agency gathers intelligence from abroad and reports it directly to the president and to the National Security Council. The CIA has special permission to be extra sneaky. For example, the director of the CIA is under no obligation to report the agency's expenditures or to reveal the size of the staff. The CIA employs many foreign agents to supply information about their own countries.

Eligibility requirements for the CIA are much the same as for the FBI. You must have a four-year college degree, preferably in electrical engineering, computer science, economics, or language (especially Chinese, Laotian, Japanese, and Korean).

One of the CIA's many programs requires you to be over thirty-five, but the rest have no age requirements. You must, however, have normal hearing, correctable 20/20 vision, and no physical defects. If they like your application, you'll go through a series of tests like the FBI. And, of course, if you pass, you still have to go through training.

———————— ◆ ————————

129. What are your chances of making it into the NBA or NFL?

College sports are the standard gateway to pro basketball and football, but the numbers are not encouraging. More than 17,600 students play NCAA Division I-A basketball and football. Each year, only *150* make it into the NBA or NFL. Most of them won't last more than one or two seasons.[1]

It would be nice to say that at least they got an education, but most don't even get that. Only 37.5 percent of college football athletes graduate; the grad rate for basketball players is 33.3 percent.[2]

GOD

130. Where did God come from?
131. Who is God?
132. Why are there so many "brands" of Christianity?
133. Who is Jesus?
134. Why doesn't God stop bad things from happening?

130. Where did God come from?

We did a genealogy on God, tracing His family tree back through history, trying to learn when and where He was born, who His parents were—*anything*. But none of the history books go back that far. There's no mention of His heritage.

Well, we did find *one* mention of it, written in a Middle Eastern book dating about the tenth century B.C. Here it is (translated into English, of course):

> Before the mountains were born
> Or you brought forth the earth and the world,
> from everlasting to everlasting you are God.*

Apparently, He's "everlasting"—infinite, no beginning and no end. Wait a minute. *Everything* has a beginning. We even celebrate this fact:

- Birthday parties (your own beginning)
- Wedding anniversaries (beginning of a marriage)
- Christmas (beginning of Jesus' life on earth)
- Fourth of July (beginning of our country)
- New Year's Day (beginning of another year)

Everything we know has an end. We make a fuss about that, too: finish lines and funerals and victory parties and closing ceremonies at the Olympics. With all this attention to beginnings and ends, it's hard to imagine something that has neither. We're familiar only with what's finite—infinity makes no sense.

And yet our finiteness is the very thing that proves *infinity*. Think about it. Everything that has a start has to have some*one* (or some*thing*) around to start it. You were started by your parents. They were started by your grandparents, who got their start from your great-grandparents, and so on. No matter how far back you take your family tree—Adam and Eve or Atom and Amoeba or Crash and Bang—*someone*

---

*The Bible, Psalm 90:2

made the very first move and started it all. And the moment He did, He invented finiteness.

If this answer makes your head spin, don't worry. You probably never will get a straight answer on this ancient question until the day you ask Him face-to-face.

◆

---

131. Who is God?

One time Moses asked God this question. God just said, "I Am." Knowing how tough it is for us humans to picture Him, God has given us some self-portraits in the Bible. Here are a few of these pictures:

God Is an Artist
The heavens declare the glory of God;
the skies proclaim the work of his hands. (Psalm 19:1).

God Is a Dad
How great is the love the Father has lavished on us, that we should be called children of God! And that is what we are! (1 John 3:1).

God Is a Doctor
He heals the brokenhearted
and binds up their wounds (Psalm 147:3).

God Is a Fortress
The LORD is a refuge for the oppressed,
a stronghold in times of trouble (Psalm 9:9).

God Is a Genius
Among all the wise men of the nations
and in all their kingdoms,
there is no one like you (Jeremiah 10:7).

God Is a Guide

I will lead the blind by ways they have not known,
along unfamiliar paths I will guide them;
I will turn the darkness into light before them
and make the rough places smooth.
(Isaiah 42:16).

God Is a King

I am the LORD, your Holy One,
Israel's Creator, your King
(Isaiah 43:15).

God Is a Listener

Before they call I will answer;
while they are still speaking I will hear
(Isaiah 65:24).

God Is a Mom

As a mother comforts her child,
so will I comfort you
(Isaiah 66:13).

◆

132. Why are there so many "brands" of Christianity?

Unlike most other religions, from the very start Christianity didn't limit itself to people of one race, culture, country, or language. In the two thousand years it's been around, it has become a part of just about every culture on the planet. These cultures add their own traditions and styles of worship. So churches that started in Germany are different from those that started in Italy or China or the southern U.S.

Some differences in churches come from disagreements in the way a church should be structured. Some churches have a formal hierarchy: the Roman Catholic church has many levels from priest to pope. Other churches have little or no hierarchy—just a preacher and a few others who manage things.

Churches may disagree about the way the worship service ought to be conducted. For example, some have Communion every Sunday; others have it once a month or so. They may also disagree about a specific reference in the Bible, like whether a woman can be a pastor or not.

From the outside, it can all look pretty confusing. But in a way, it's great. Wouldn't it be horrible if everyone had to worship Jesus in exactly the same way—sing all the same songs (in Dutch, let's say), pray the same prayers (all long ones), and believe exactly the same thing on every little issue?

Instead, we have millions and millions of people all over the planet who celebrate their love for Jesus in a thousand different ways.

◆

133. Who Is Jesus?

You already know that He was a Jewish carpenter and teacher who lived in what is now the country of Israel. Christians also believe that He was God, born as a baby. It's a wild idea when you stop to think about it.

God, Creator of the universe, King of the entire world, makes His grand entrance onto earth as a thumb-sucking, dirty-diapered infant born in a barn (hence, His habit of forgetting to shut doors—just kidding). It makes you wonder. Was God thinking clearly when He came up with this idea? Why did God choose such an unimpressive entrance into our lives?

The reason is this: God wasn't trying to impress, astound, or amaze us. He was trying to tell us that He loves us. Sure, He could have spelled out *I love you* in the clouds or hung autographed posters of Himself everywhere with captions that read *I love you!* But God wanted to tell us face-to-face.

Which led to a problem: God's face is so intensely brilliant, you'd *melt* just by looking at it (kind of like staring at a nuclear explosion). And if He spoke to you (just before your ears dripped off), His voice might burst your eardrums and explode your heart. We humans weren't designed to survive such magnificence. He had to find another way. His solution? Join the human race.

If He became a human, we could see and hear and touch Him—without fear of combustion. So that's what He did. Jesus didn't just drop out of the sky *disguised* as a human. He *was* a human, and He arrived here just like everyone else. He even had a belly button to prove it.

While Jesus was on the earth, He told people that He loved them. But He also showed them: He listened to their problems, spent time with nerds and crazies, and healed people wherever He went. Face-to-face, He told them all about God's love. No one melted.

As a real-life human, God got to experience the joys of humanity firsthand: laughter, sunsets, back rubs, dinner with dessert, late-night conversations with friends around a fire, the way the air smells after it rains.

But He also got to taste the bitter stuff: diaper rash, stubbed toes, smashed thumbs, splinters under the fingernail, boring teachers, rejection from friends, loneliness, being beaten up, hatred, temptation, wicked people, hunger, thirst, murder. He is not some distant and unknowable Force who is so different from us that He can't relate. He has eaten, laughed, cried, and bled—just like you. He has been in your shoes; He knows what it's like.

One person put it this way: "For we do not have a high priest who is unable to sympathize with our weaknesses, but we have one who has been tempted in every way, just as we are—yet was without sin. Let us then approach the throne of grace with confidence, so that we may receive mercy and find grace to help us in our time of need."*

So what does this mean for *you*? You can call out God's name. You can talk to Him directly. And you can do it without

---

*Hebrews 4:15–16

bursting into flames. All because the almighty God, Creator of the universe, King of kings, Knower of all things, showed up in His birthday suit one night awhile back. What an entrance.

———————— ◆ ————————

134. Why doesn't God stop bad things from happening?

God doesn't run the world like a person operating a miniature train set. He doesn't control our actions or compel us to think or believe or act only in ways that please Him. He shows His love for us by allowing our lives to "happen"—the good and the bad, choices wise and unwise.

"But no one chooses to get cancer," you say. Yes, but if God took away all the bad stuff, He would, in essence, control us. Why bother to exert any control over your own life when you know that nothing bad can come of it? God doesn't fix the game so that you win automatically.

—Jobs—

135. How do you find a job?
136. How do you prepare a resume?
137. How do you make a good first impression with a potential employer?
138. What kinds of questions will a potential employer ask? How do you answer?
139. What do you do to make your job interview a success?
140. When do you know it's the right time to quit a job?
141. Is there a right way to quit?
142. You'd like to start your own business. What are some ideas?
143. What do you need to do to get your business off the ground?

135. How do you find a job?

Most people check the newspaper and the job board at school. But if jobs are scarce in your community, you may have to be more creative in your search. Here are some methods that work:

Get Connected If an employer has a choice, she'll hire someone she knows (or at least someone who knows someone she knows) before hiring a complete stranger. Ask your parents if they have any friends who own businesses or can somehow help you find a job where they work. Ask your friends about open positions they know about.

Trade Places If you have a friend who is getting ready to quit a good job, you may be able to take his place. You'll still have to sell yourself to the boss, but you've already got one foot in the door.

Open Up Apply to a business that's about to open. For example, if you see a storefront being remodeled, ask the contractor or property manager for the name and address of the owner. Send her a letter and a resume, and follow up with a phone call. Showing this kind of initiative may be all you need to get the job.

Check Out Job Lists Employers advertise for jobs in other places besides the want ads. The Chamber of Commerce may list summer job opportunities in your area. The Labor Department's U.S. Employment Service has offices in many cities throughout the country that list jobs in the area—call them by finding the number in the government section of the phone book. Many YMCAs, churches, and other community organizations sponsor job boards listing part-time and summer jobs open to teenagers.

Go to College To look at the job board, at least. Employers who can afford to pay higher wages for part-time help will go after college students; they hope to get workers more

reliable and mature than high schoolers. So, they often advertise on job boards at the local college. Just remember: when
you apply for one of these jobs, you'll have to prove you're as
reliable and mature as any college student they're likely to
hire.

Work for Free   Some jobs are worth going through drastic
measures to get. Lots of students are willing to take a nonpaid
internship just to get a foot in the door. If you're a hard
worker and a paid position eventually opens up, you're in the
ideal place for it. To get an internship on your own, introduce
yourself to the manager, owner, or professional you want to
work for. Tell her you are eager to work for no pay in ex-
change for the training and experience. If the employer
senses that you're sincerely interested in the opportunity and
not a vulture hovering around until someone quits, dies, or
gets fired, he may take you on.

◆

136. How do you prepare a resume?

Most jobs for teenagers don't require one, but preparing one
is always a good idea because you take an inventory of your
skills. Even if you never show it to anyone, it can build your
confidence by convincing you that you have skills that employers want. Here's how to build a resume:

1. Write down every job experience you've ever had, from
    delivering papers to baby-sitting to selling Girl Scout
    cookies to sweeping floors at your Uncle Elmo's lamp-
    shade store.
2. Include other experiences that have prepared you for
    working: sports accomplishments, club involvement,
    talents such as playing a musical instrument or program-
    ming a computer.
3. Under each of these jobs and experiences, list the *skills*
    you learned because of it. For example, if you baby-sat,

your skills might be working with children and developing trust with grown-ups. If you've been playing the violin for five years, you know what dedication is all about.

4. Quantify your experiences. Put down the number of boxes of cookies you sold and how that compared to the rest of your troop. List the number of tournaments you planned as president of the hackisack club.

After completing all these notes, you're ready to write the real resume. Since a list of your "real" job experiences might fit onto an index card, organize your resume by *skills* instead of *jobs*. The skills might be...

- Work Well with Others (and a list of experiences that prove this).
- Organization and Leadership (include leadership positions, accomplishments, activities).
- Sales Experience (what you've sold, how much, how long).

At the bottom of the resume you can mention other accomplishments, hobbies, awards, and interests that shed light on the kind of person you are. The most important thing to remember is that an employer isn't looking for someone with a ton of experience—that's why she's hiring a *student*. Your goal is to convince her that the few experiences you *have* had will make you more valuable to her.

———————◆———————

137. How do you make a good first impression with a potential employer?

First impressions are often wrong. But when you're hunting for a job, you can't afford to make a bad one because you won't be around to correct it. Here are a few tips to help you make the right impression:

Clothing   Wear what you'd wear on the job if you were hired. If you're unsure, it's better to overdress than underdress. But make sure you feel comfortable—if you *feel* strange, you *look* strange.

Hair   Fix it so that it stays out of your eyes. Compulsive adults will be thinking of how to shove it out of the way for you and will miss what you're saying.

Smell   Don't. That means no body odor and not a lot of cologne, perfume, or aftershave. (Hint: if they smell you before they see you, it's too much.) Try not to smell like tobacco, gasoline, or a wet dog. And use a breath mint.

Makeup   Avoid makeup that looks like it was applied while you were riding on a motorcycle. This is especially important for girls.

Handshake   Offer to shake hands when you meet: age and sex don't matter. Give a firm, friendly grip, look into the person's eyes, and smile. *(*Translation: *"Meeting you is important to me.")*

Eyes   Look directly at the person's face when you speak. *("I believe in what I'm saying.")* Do the same when you're listening to people. *("I care about what you're saying.")*

Nose   Don't put paper clips in your nose. *("I can be trusted with office supplies.")*

Conversation   Your ability to communicate is being evaluated. When meeting, state your name clearly (if the person has forgotten your name, you save her the embarrassment of having to ask). Address an adult by his or her last name (e.g., Mr. Rogers or Ms. Piggy) until you're given permission to use the first name. Use the name frequently—people like to hear their names.

———————— ◆ ————————

138. What kinds of questions will a potential employer ask? How do you answer?

Every employer has a different style, but most tend to ask some of these questions:

Question	Answer
Tell me about yourself.	Make it short and sweet: your school, grade, family, interests.
What subjects do you enjoy? Why?	Be honest. Show enthusiasm over things you like.
Sports? Hobbies? Other interests?	Again, show enthusiasm and a sense of dedication for the things you care about.
Do you drive? Own a car?	What he's really asking: "Can you be counted on to get here on time?" and "Can you run errands that require driving?" If you don't have a car, assure him that you have a reliable means of getting to work.
What are your strengths?	What he *wants* to hear: "I work hard and learn fast. I'm reliable." If it's true, say it.
What are your weaknesses?	"Acceptable" weaknesses mean you have too much of a good thing: you are a perfectionist, too task oriented, overly self-critical.
What are your future plans?	*Anything* ambitious sounds better than "I don't really know."
What days and hours can you work?	Have a copy of your schedule; be honest about nonnegotiables—school, study, church, family time.

Why do you want to work here? It's a good place to work, challenging, nice coworkers, good reputation, quality product—say whatever is true.

◆

139. What do you do to make your job interview a success?

Here are a few tips from employers:

- Convey what makes you *unique*. You want to be *remembered*.
- Show interest in the *job*, not the *compensation*.
- Remember that employers *don't expect teenagers to be experts* when they hire them.
- They're looking for *enthusiasm, eagerness to learn, a cooperative spirit*, and *reliability*. If you can get that message across in your interview, you've done the best you can.
- Every interview is a priceless lesson: take notes, *learn from your mistakes*, look back and laugh, and get better.
- Never start a *water balloon fight* during a job interview (but if someone else throws the first balloon, go for the kill).

◆

140. When do you know it's the right time to quit a job?

A job can be a great thing to have, but it can also be the last thing you need right now. Every semester you need to ask yourself the same question: Do the pressures and conflicts, as well as less time for studying, friendships, family, and other activities, outweigh the benefits of money and experience?

If so, it's time to quit. You'll have the opportunity (some call it a curse) of working for most of the rest of your life. But all the money in the world can't buy back the time lost with family, friends, and studies.

Even if the job fits into your schedule and priorities, there may be other reasons to quit.

- You have an unresolvable conflict with a boss or co-worker.
- You're forced to work under unsafe conditions.
- You're moving to Tasmania.
- You or your employer is doing something you believe is immoral or illegal.
- Coworkers are having a negative influence on your behavior or attitude.
- You're being sexually or physically harassed.
- You've found a job that suits your needs better.

Whatever your reasons, write out all the positive and negative aspects of the job. The next time you look for a job, you can review the list and avoid getting yourself into a similar situation.

———————— ◆ ————————

141. Is there a right way to quit?

Yes. Here are a few tips:

- Make sure your boss hears the news from you, not a coworker.
- Be prepared to give a reason. If it's money, be ready for the possibility that you'll be offered more.
- If you've found a better job, tell her. If the reasons it's better are beyond her control (closer to home, related to

your career goals), let her know so she won't feel person-ally responsible.

• If you're quitting because you can't stand her, it's best to hold your tongue. Arguing about her faults won't get you anywhere. In fact, it may do you harm. She may give you a bad recommendation for a future job or take it out on any of your friends who still work there.

• Give two weeks' notice so she can find and train a re-placement. But just because you give her two weeks doesn't mean she has to return the favor. If she finds someone right away or you start acting like most people do when they know they're leaving, she'll let you go.

———————— ◆ ————————

142. You'd like to start your own business. What are some ideas?

Rent a Chef. Hire yourself out to neighbors who don't have time to cook and clean up the dishes but would like an excellent meal prepared in their homes.

Really Fresh Foods. Make your own peanut butter, apple pies, cookies, or candies. Package and sell them to neighbors and local stores.

Personal Shopper. Some adults are too busy to stand in line at the supermarket or drive all over town looking for a vacuum cleaner part. Do their shopping for them.

Go to Town Errands. Same idea, but you'll run any errand: pick up clothes at the cleaners, stand in line at the DMV, take the dog to the vet.

KidLimo. Be a kid driver. Pick the kids up after school; drop one at the day-care center and another at baseball practice, and take the third to the dentist.

Dog Gone Walking. Offer memberships to your daily dog

walking service, with washing and brushing on Saturdays. Also offer pet sitting to owners who're going out of town.

Two Wheel Tune. Offer tune-ups, flat repairs, adjustments, and detailing—and you pick up and deliver.

Friday Flowers. Sell once-a-week flower delivery to homes. Buy the flowers from a wholesaler. Arrange and deliver them to your clients' homes every Friday.

Hired Pen. If you're a calligrapher, sell your penmanship to people who need to create or address invitations, Christmas cards, or nametags.

Mr. Bills. Stop by your clients' houses once a week to organize their bills, write checks for them to sign, mail the payments, file the statements, and balance their checkbooks.

Maximum Memories. Put together photo albums for people who take lots of pictures but never seem to have the time to organize them. Create schoolwork scrapbooks for their kids.

Proper Places. Organize people's kitchens, drawers, desks, albums, videos, files, offices, closets, pantries, and garages. Offer package deals and monthly maintenance contracts.

Party Performances. Perform as a clown or magician for children's parties.

KidVids. Offer to videotape birthday parties, bar mitzvahs, recitals, plays, and sporting events. If you don't have a camera, see if you can borrow or rent one from school or a camera store.

Professor Tutor. Tutor kids in subjects you enjoy.

Just My Type. Type reports for high-school and college students.

Page by Page. If you have access to a computer, laser printer, and desktop publishing software, offer to create fliers and mailings for small businesses.

———————— ◆ ————————

143. What do you need to do to get your business off the ground?

Lots of people have a great idea for a business. They pour their time and money into the scheme only to find out that the business will never work. Here are some of the questions entrepreneurs ask themselves when considering a new business:

The Need   What need will your business fill? If you can't describe it in one sentence, you'll have a tough time selling the idea to others.

The Market   Who are your potential customers? How many are there? How much will they pay for your product or service?

The Money   What will it cost you to launch the business? How much will it cost to keep it going? How many customers can you expect? What's the minimum you'll need to stay afloat?

The Legal Stuff   Will you need a business license? Do you need any other kinds of permits? Will you need insurance?

The Commitment   How much time will it take? Can you afford the time away from studies, family, friends, and other commitments?

The Reward   Why are you doing this? What will you get out of it financially?

Talk through your answers with someone who's launched a business, such as a family member or a friend's parent. Have that person ask you more questions. After doing this homework, if you still think you can pull it off, go for it.

——LAW——

144. Why are there so many rules?

Most adults forget how many rules are specifically designed to regulate the life of a teenager:

- Curfew
- Child labor laws
- Truancy
- Loitering
- Driving restrictions
- Drinking age limits
- Laws on buying tobacco
- Marriage restrictions
- R ratings on movies
- Voting age
- Contract enforcement
- Contest rules
- School rules

Most rules are there for good reasons—your education, physical safety, or protection from unscrupulous adults. But rules are rules: they remind you of what you *can't* do. Maybe there should be *another* rule: anytime adults make a rule about something you can't do, they have to list all the things you *can* do. At least that would remind us that *most* things still are legal.

Sometimes it's easier to appreciate your situation when you find out how bad off other people are. In Singapore, a wealthy island nation in Asia, they have strictly enforced rules for *everyone*.

Crime	Punishment
Jaywalking	$30
Driving without a seat belt	$124
Eating food on the subway	$310
Smoking in a restaurant	$310
Not flushing a public toilet	$620

Urinating in an elevator	Up to $1,240 and your photo in the newspaper

Which seems mild when you realize that in some Muslim countries, thieves can have a hand cut off.

◆

145. What happens when you're arrested?

When you're arrested, you're taken to the police station for processing.

- A check for prior convictions is completed.
- A file is created on you.
- A police photo is taken: front, back, profile.
- You're fingerprinted.

If the offense is severe, you're taken to a juvenile facility, and your parents are contacted. If the offense isn't severe, you may be released to your parents. If you're detained at the juvenile hall, you're given a "detention" hearing within forty-eight hours of your arrest to figure out if they can keep you locked up.

Then there's a "readiness" hearing to determine if your case should go to trial. If so, you're tried in a "dispositional" hearing.

◆

146. What happens if you're stopped for driving under the influence?

Each year in the U.S., over one million people are arrested for driving under the influence (DUI). Despite all these arrests, twenty-five thousand humans die and half a million are seriously injured in alcohol-related traffic accidents. Each year.

Figuring that being arrested for DUI is better than crashing and dying—or crashing and killing—the "lucky" ones can look forward to the following events.*

If the police pull you over and smell alcohol on your breath, the officer may immediately seize your driver's license—*instant* suspension of driving privileges. The officer may give you a street sobriety test, or he or she may take you to the police station; your car is towed away (and you get to pay the towing bill).

At the station you're given a choice of three tests to figure out your blood alcohol concentration (BAC): breath, urine, or blood sample. In some states, if you refuse to take the test, they lock you up. In other states (California, for one) blood is taken from you forcibly: they strap you down to a table and draw blood. If the BAC test says you weren't intoxicated, you're given the traffic ticket for whatever you were originally pulled over for; then you're free to go.

If the test says you were intoxicated, you're held until a parent comes to claim you. If a parent can't be reached (or decides not to come), you're put in the juvenile detention facility until a parent gets you out. You go to court within thirty days.

In court the judge can do all sorts of things to you, depending on the circumstances. You may get hit with any combination of the following: longer loss of driving privileges, fines, juvenile detention, jail, community service, traffic school, alcohol education classes. On top of that, you'll pay horrendous insurance premiums and possibly get stuck with a substantial bill from your attorney. And there's an arrest on your record.

The saddest part about all this is that we the people have had to concoct such nasty consequences to stop people from drinking and driving. You'd think that the possibility of killing someone's dad or mom or kid would be deterrent enough.

◆

*DUI laws differ from state to state. This is what happens in California—most states have similar laws.

147. What do stores do when they catch shoplifters?

It depends on the situation. Sometimes the clerk, manager, or security person will call a minor's parents and ask them to pick up their child. Usually, however, the person will call the police.

The store has a right to detain you if it determines that there was an "intent to steal." That means different things in different states. In some places, you must leave the store with an unpurchased item. In others, all you have to do is conceal the article—wear it beneath your clothes, or put it in your purse or bag. In some states, you can show "intent to steal" just by leaving the *floor or department* with an unpurchased item. Busted.

The store now has the right to detain you until the police arrive. The officer takes you to the police station and contacts your parents. If they can be reached, you're booked and detained until they arrive. If they cannot be reached, you may be sent to a juvenile facility and kept there until a parent claims you.

How Stores Catch You   Retailers lose many millions of dollars each year to shoplifters, so they can afford clever ways to catch shoplifters. The larger the store, the more high-tech stuff they use:

- Plainclothes security people wandering the aisles
- Hidden video cameras monitored by a security person with lots of TV screens
- Two-way mirrors *everywhere*—some with cameras behind them, others with real people (so the next time you stop at a mirrored post to pick your teeth, remember that you may be on stage)
- Security tags that set off detectors at the door
- Locked dressing rooms; clerks trained to count the number of items you carry in and out

◆

148. Can a police officer shoot you?

Generally, a police officer will fire a gun for only three reasons:

1. The officer is in a kill-or-be-killed or wound-or-be-wounded situation (in other words, in self-defense).
2. Another officer is in danger.
3. A citizen is in danger of being killed.

So if it *appears* to an officer that you are about to wound or kill someone, he or she may shoot you. It's a judgment call, often made in the worst of conditions. Police officers train and train to be able to make the right call in every circumstance. Tragically, every once in a while they call it wrong, and some kid with a toy gun or a teenager reaching inside his coat gets shot.

How to Keep from Getting Shot If you're on the street, at a party, or in a car and an officer stops you, avoid doing anything that may appear threatening. Be cool and cooperative. The officer just wants to be able to go home that night in one piece.

- Don't run away.
- If you're holding a bottle, a can, a tool, or anything else that might hurt if it hit someone, set it down.
- Don't make quick movements or reach into a coat, purse, or drawer.
- Don't joke around.
- Obviously, don't reach for the officer.
- If you're being searched and you have a pocket knife in your pocket or purse, tell the officer (officers don't like surprises).
- If you're pulled over in a car—especially at night—put both hands on the steering wheel so the officer knows you're not holding anything. If you're a passenger, just put your hands in your lap. Don't reach under the seat unless you're asked to do so.

149. Can the police search you, your car, or your house without a warrant?

Definitely. To justify a search, a police officer need have only *probable cause*—a strong suspicion of wrongdoing. For example, if an officer or a citizen reports seeing something illegal through a window, a police officer can enter, search, and seize without a warrant. The same is true if chasing a fleeing felon leads an officer into a home.

Without probable cause, an officer needs a warrant to search anything not clearly seen. But if you're hiding something, you're still not off the hook. Thanks to modern technology such as cellular phones and fax machines, the officer may be able to get a warrant in a couple of hours.

———————— ◆ ————————

150. Can the police listen in on your phone conversations?

As strange as it seems, it depends on what kind of phone you're using. If you're talking on a regular telephone that plugs into the wall, an officer needs the court's permission to set up a wiretap. That's because the phone line is considered private property and is subject to the laws on search and seizure.

But if you're talking on a cordless or cellular phone, these laws don't apply. Why not? Because wireless phones convey the call through radio waves, which are considered public property in the U.S. By the way, if you use a cordless phone at home, any neighbor with a simple radio scanner can listen in. So say nice things about them and refrain from making those smooching noises when you say good-bye to people.

———————— ◆ ————————

151. Is it legal to carry a gun or a knife?

Laws on weapons vary from state to state and even city to city, but here's what's typical:

Knives   A blade that's three inches or longer can't be concealed. That means you can't carry a hunting knife in your pocket, purse, or bookbag. Switchblades of any size are also illegal.

Handguns   It's illegal to carry a handgun without a permit, which you can't get unless you're at least eighteen years old. Even if you have a permit to *carry* a gun, you may not *conceal* it unless your permit says so.

◆

152. What happens to your criminal record when you turn eighteen?

Many people believe that when you turn eighteen, your record is automatically sealed. But that is not the case.* Your record is *archived,* which means that it's filed away and that you begin a clean file as an adult. As an adult, if you're ever accused of a crime, a judge decides whether your juvenile file can be unarchived—viewed and considered in the case. To get your record *sealed,* you must make a specific request to do so. You can't do that until you're eighteen; if you've been committed to the youth authority, you might have to wait until you're twenty-one. If you committed a felony as a minor but were tried as an adult, you can't seal your record.

If your record is sealed, no one may reopen the file: you've

---

*This information describes what happens in California and many other states; the rules in your state may be different.

got a clean slate. As far as the authorities are concerned, your previous offenses have ceased to exist. You don't have to admit them on any applications or to anyone who asks.

◆

153. What does it mean to be tried as an adult?

It means that the crime you're being accused of is severe enough to deserve adult punishment. In the eyes of the law, adult crimes deserve adult punishments. For example, if you're convicted of murder as a minor, the maximum sentencing is usually five years. As an adult, you could get life. Once you're tried as an adult, the law treats you as an adult—all your rights as a minor disappear.

◆

154. What are child labor laws, and how do they affect you?

Jack London, the man who wrote *The Call of the Wild*, held some tough jobs as a teenager about 100 years ago. When he was fifteen, he worked at a cannery ten hours a day for a dollar a day.

Nowadays, to protect you from such horrible work, the government has strict laws about how many hours you can work and the kinds of jobs you can do. The Fair Labor Standards Act is the federal law affecting anyone under eighteen. It says that you can't work during school hours or perform dangerous work—operate meat slicing machines, work on scaffolding, perform tiger tonsillectomies, stuff like that.

If you're under sixteen, the rules are even more restrictive: you can't work more than three hours on a school day, work past seven at night, or put in more than eighteen hours during the week.

Each state has its own labor laws, which may be stricter than the federal law. For example, the state may require that you get a work permit. You can get the facts by talking to a school counselor or by contacting the state employment or labor office in your area.

———————— ◆ ————————

155. How do you change your name?

In states which use common law, you can usually change your name just by using the new name consistently in your personal and business life. You must be at least eighteen. The preferred method in all states, however, is by judicial decree.

In California, if you're under eighteen, you have to do it by petition, which requires you to

- complete a few forms and file them with the applicable court along with a petition, which must be signed by one of your parents or your legal guardian. If both parents are deceased and you have no legal guardian, a relative or friend may sign it.

- publish a short notice in the newspaper directing all interested persons to appear in court at the specified date to show cause why the application should not be granted (it appears in the classifieds in the legal notice section that you've always wondered about).

- pay a fee ($70 to $140 in California).

———————— ◆ ————————

156. Can you legally change your name to anything you want?

No. A judge will check your name choice to see if it's legal and decent. Here are some names that may not work:

- An obscene or offensive name.
- A number or anything else that's confusing (so 007 won't work).
- A name protected by a copyright or trademark if you plan to make money with the name. For example, if you're a rock musician, you're not going to be able to choose Ronald McDonald, Mickey Mouse, or Spiderman.
- The name of a famous person—if you plan to make money with it. The person doesn't even have to be alive. In California, for example, the person's heirs can protect the name for fifty years. Forget about Humphrey Bogart or Elvis Presley.

You *can* choose a one-word name if you like: Cher and Bono (of U2) did.

———————— ◆ ————————

157. What's emancipation? How do you do it?

Emancipation is the process of releasing yourself from your parents' authority. Minors who feel that they will have better control over their lives may petition for this. It's most common among foster and group-home teenagers who would like to move out on their own. Here's the process:

- You must be at least fourteen years old. It differs from state to state, but fourteen is the youngest age.
- You must show some legal means of support, such as a steady job or an inheritance, and that you are managing your own finances.

- You must prove that you are willingly living apart from a consenting parent or guardian.
- You fill out petition papers for the court. If it looks like you have what it takes, a court date is set.
- You meet with a judge who considers all the facts and decides whether to grant emancipation.

Once you're emancipated, you're free and clear of your parents' authority. For the most part, you gain the same rights as an adult of eighteen—you can stay out after curfew, be arrested as an adult, and make decisions as an adult. You'll still be restricted by some age laws, such as driving, drinking, and voting.

——— LEARNING ———

158. What's IQ?

Intelligence quotient is your mental age divided by your chronological age multiplied by 100. If you're ten years old but mentally function on the level of a twelve-year-old, your IQ will be 12/10 x 100, or 120.

Your mental age can be determined by a test appropriate for your age. Schools use the results of these tests to place students in special programs (both gifted and challenged). Here are the breakdowns for IQ:

Above 140	Near genius or genius
130–40	Very superior
120–29	Superior
110–19	High average (formerly "bright")
90–109	Average
80–89	Low average (formerly "dull")
70–79	Borderline
69 and less	Mentally deficient

Generally, anyone scoring 120 or above would enter a gifted program. Students scoring 70 or below would qualify for special education classes.

◆

159. Does cramming work?

If your goal is to remember a whole bunch of material only for as long as it takes to get through a test, cramming works. In the adult world, cramming is actually a useful skill.

- Business executives cram before critical meetings.
- Salespeople cram for important presentations.
- Reporters cram before doing special interviews.
- Attorneys cram for trials.
- Performers cram for auditions and big performances.
- Musicians cram before recording sessions and concerts.

The information they cram into their brains is specific stuff that they need to know only for a short time. The problem with cramming in *school* is that much of what you learn is general knowledge that you're going to need all your life: math, science, language, and social skills.

When you cram *these* subjects, your brain never has time to absorb the information. You may pass the test this week, but in a few years you may discover that you failed in a bigger way. All the people who actually *learned* the stuff—who know how to work with numbers, communicate with words, and comprehend complex concepts (and compound sentences)—have become the bosses and business owners and decision makers and world changers.

Meanwhile, the ones who didn't learn these essentials sit around wondering why they don't like their jobs, get paid so poorly, and fail to accomplish their goals. But, hey, at least they got an *A* on the test.

Much of what you learn in school will never be used later on. But a lot of it *will*. And unless you've figured out a way to fast-forward the tape of your life to see what you'll need to know, it's safest to study for the long term. If nothing else, you can use it to help your own kids study.

———————— ◆ ————————

160. How can you study better?

You already know how to study better. Just study as if you *want* to learn the material.

Get a Front Row Seat If you've ever watched a horror film from the first row in a theater, you know that being close to the action is a memorable experience. Likewise, sitting closer to the teacher helps you concentrate harder and remember more. Some students jump one whole grade just by moving up close.

Catch the Preview   Movie theaters show previews to interest you in coming back to see the whole film. In the same way, reading the study material *before* it's discussed in class can interest you in the lesson. (If nothing else, you can check the teacher for errors.)

Write It Down   When the person of your dreams finally gives you his or her phone number, you write it down...and the act of writing helps you memorize it. For most people, taking notes dramatically increases their recollection of the information—even if they never read the notes. (A few people actually do worse when they take notes—if you're one of them, you know it.)

Watch the Rerun   Have you ever watched a movie or TV show a second time and discovered a whole bunch of things you missed the first time? Read the follow-up material and your class notes. You'll catch stuff you missed in the lesson, some of which may even be interesting.

————————— ◆ —————————

161. How do you know if you have a learning disability? What can you do about it?

A learning-disabled person is anyone with math, spelling, or reading disabilities. (A reading disability is also known as dyslexia.) One in ten students may have an undiagnosed learning disability.[1] The study of this problem is pretty new so there's no surefire way of detecting everyone who may be afflicted. The range of disabilities includes ADD (attention deficit disorder or hyperactivity) and SED (severely emotionally disturbed)—they're big on three-letter names.

If you're having problems in at least two learning areas, especially reading, you may want to ask your school counselor to test you for a disability. The testing process may qualify you for extra help.

Another excellent way to combat a learning disability is to work with a personal tutor. Studies show that this is the best method with ADD students. Private tutoring can be an expensive alternative, but many schools have excellent peer tutoring programs or after-school programs that are free. If your school doesn't offer a similar program, suggest that one be started.

——LOVE——

162. How do you keep a relationship healthy?
163. How do you tell someone "I love you"?
164. How do you write a love poem?
165. Is there a right way to kiss?
166. How do you break up with someone?
167. Your friends talk about girls constantly, but you're not really interested in them yet. Is there something wrong with you? Is everyone else normal? Are you the only one who doesn't think about girls constantly? Are you afraid? Are you ugly? Will you ever think of girls? Are you gay? Are you from another planet? Are you normal?
168. Why are guys so obnoxious, insensitive, and rude?

162. How do you keep a relationship healthy?

In his book *Next Time I Fall in Love,** youth worker Chap Clark claims that most relationships get out of whack when they don't grow equally in six key areas:

- Emotional
- Physical
- Social
- Intellectual
- Spiritual
- Degree of commitment

In the beginning of the relationship, things are fine because the depth in all these areas is equal—and shallow. But as the relationship grows, the first three areas—emotional, physical, and social—start to outpace the last three. Many couples who have a pretty good relationship for the first month or so look back six months later and wonder what happened. They used to talk; now they make out.

Sit down with your partner and chart out your relationship. How much time and effort do you put into each of these areas? Then draw a chart that represents what you'd like the relationship to look like. What's it going to take to get from the first chart to the second? Agree on some goals to get you there.

—————————— ◆ ——————————

*Chap Clark, *Next Time I Fall in Love* (Grand Rapids, MI: Zondervan, 1987).

163. How do you tell someone "I love you"?

Here are a few ideas adapted from *Creative Dating:**

- Send it in a telegram.
- Fax it.
- Weave it into his tennis racket.
- Spell it in jelly beans or green M&Ms.
- Write it with birdseed on his lawn.
- Give her an I Love You balloon.
- Train a parrot to say it (or buy one that already knows how).
- Carve it in balsa wood and float it in the toilet.
- Hire an airplane to pull an I Love You banner. If you see someone else's, claim it as your own.
- Shave it into the back of his hair.
- Trim it into his hedge (make sure you have the right address).
- Inscribe it on the inside of her sunglasses.
- Say it in sign language.
- Bake it into a fortune cookie.
- Brand it on his polo pony.

◆

---

164. How do you write a love poem?

It doesn't have to rhyme. It doesn't have to be gushy or drippy or get you an *A* in creative writing class. Tracy Green, TV producer and occasional writer of love poems, has a simple formula.

Creative Dating by Doug Fields and Todd Temple (Nashville: Oliver-Nelson, 1986).

Write the word *YOU* at the top and bottom of a piece of paper. In between, just list any words at all that come to mind when you think of the person: images, colors, moments, emotions. Don't even think about rhyme or rhythm—there's absolutely no such thing as doing this wrong. Here's an example:

> YOU
> delight
> brilliant
> quick thoughts
> perfect letters
> beautiful
> laughter
> YOU

What could possibly be more simple? Try one.

◆

165. Is there a right way to kiss?

No. Everyone has his or her own style. Kind of like fingerprints, no two are alike (but unlike fingerprints, the FBI doesn't keep *kiss* files). The only two things you can do to take the pizzazz out of a kiss are (1) to make your mouth tense and (2) to freeze up.

Relax your mouth so your partner can feel flesh, not Formica. Then move your mouth a little—kisses are motion pictures, not freeze frames.

◆

166. How do you break up with someone?

Chances are pretty good that if you're dating someone, sooner or later you're going to want to *stop* dating. If your partner is the one who drops you, it hurts. If you're the one who does the dropping, it hurts (although not as much). Is there any solution to this yucky situation? No—but there are some things you can do to make it a little less yucky.

Don't...

Put it off. Your partner can usually figure out something's wrong. Stringing the person along or forcing a guessing game doesn't do either of you any good.

Make it a trial. You may be tempted to go on the attack: "It's your fault! You're a jerk! You blew it!" You, you, you. Although these things may be true, the other person doesn't need to hear it that way. Explain your feelings and decisions, not your partner's. Losing you is enough to deal with—there's no need to destroy an ego, too.

Say, "Just friends." It cheapens friendships and doesn't make the letdown any easier.

Do...

Decide. There's only one thing worse than breaking up, and that's staying in a dating relationship that is hurting you or compromising your morals. Sit down and deal with it.

Make it clean. Don't confuse the person by breaking up, then calling when you're lonely, bored, or need an ego boost. If those are the only times you miss the person, breaking up was the right thing to do.

Take the lesson. Take time to figure out why the relationship ended—and what you'll do different the next time.

———————— ◆ ————————

167. Your friends talk about girls constantly, but you're not really interested in them yet. Is there something wrong with you? Is everyone else normal? Are you the only one who doesn't think about girls constantly? Are you afraid? Are you ugly? Will you ever think of girls? Are you gay? Are you from another planet? Are you normal?

Yes, you're normal.

A large but silent percentage of teenagers doesn't date or fall in love until after graduating from high school. Most are normal, healthy, good-looking people who either aren't interested in dating yet or haven't met anyone they care to get involved with. They're not as conspicuous as their dating peers because they don't announce their condition (HEY, EVERYONE—I'VE NEVER BEEN KISSED—I'M NOT EVEN SURE I LIKE GIRLS). They prefer to just relax, let nature take its course, and concentrate on the things important to them.

You're Not Immature   Maturity in life means acting your age. Some guys pretend to be interested in girls way before they actually are, just so they can fit in. Don't fall into the trap of doing stuff before it's time just because some of your friends have arrived there first. When you're ripe for romance, you'll know it—and it'll be that much sweeter because you waited.

Your Body Knows What It's Doing   Your body doesn't look at your birth certificate to figure out when it's time for you to start puberty. Nor does it look at the armpit hair on all your friends and say, "Okay, hormones, wake up and get to work."

Some of your friends may look like they've been shaving since kindergarten. Others can put off buying a jock strap until college. If puberty hits you later than most, take heart. People who reach puberty early are more likely to have premature sexual relationships that can mess up their love life later on.

Your Time Will Come   Some guys freak out when they realize that they're not interested in girls. *Does that mean you'll never be interested in girls?*

No. Romantic relationships are wild and complicated contraptions. Good ones are possible only when all the pieces are in place. Adolescence is the factory: your mind, emotions, desires, and social skills are being formed and fitted together in order to make healthy relationships. When all these areas are properly developed, the desire will come.

If you're not interested in girls, it just means you're not ready for a romantic relationship *right now*. It also means that God is still shaping and fitting things, so you'll be ready when your time comes.

You Can Be a Better Friend   All too soon you'll realize how tough it is to have a good friendship with some girls without that uneasy feeling that they're looking for something romantic—and you're not (or vice versa). But if you don't have much romantic interest in females right now, you'll find it easier to be yourself. You can concentrate on making good friendships with girls rather than on looking for a "girlfriend."

Later on, when love does interest you, you'll find that the best romantic relationships start with good friendships. And if you already know how to form great friendships with females, you'll be ahead in the game.

———————— ◆ ————————

168. Why are guys so obnoxious, insensitive, and rude?

There are three reasons:

They're Immature Really. On average, girls enter puberty before boys. That's why you see freshman guys who could pass for twelve-year-olds—and eighth-grade girls who turn the heads of senior guys. The trauma is so great that it takes years for them to catch up. Give them time.

They're Socially Ignorant Girls have been working at relationships for years. You talk about friendships and work through tensions among friends. Most guys are just learning to do these things, and they're not as skilled at them yet. Teach them how.

They're Hungry for Attention Many guys have a tough time establishing intimacy. Without the love and affirmation that come from intimate friendships, they go for attention in other ways. Show them how to build close friendships.

169. What's the proper way to introduce someone?

170. Is it okay to call an adult by his or her first name?

171. What do you do if you forget someone's name?

172. Your parents taught you to open doors for women, but some people say this is sexist. What's the right thing to do?

173. How should you act around a person in a wheelchair?

174. How should you act around people who are blind or deaf?

175. How do you know which utensils to use at a multi-course meal?

176. How do you stop someone from choking?

177. Why do guys leave the toilet seat up all the time?

178. Why do girls get so mad when guys leave the toilet seat up all the time?

179. What should you do when you inhale a fly?

180. What do you do if you lean against the bathroom counter and get a wet spot on your front?

181. What do you do when you're in a seat that emits a sound remarkably similar to an actual body noise?

182. Are there any discreet ways to check your zipper?

183. How do you check for body odor without drawing attention to yourself?

184. What do you do if you're discovered with a portion of your dress tucked into your pantyhose?

185. What do you do when people notice that a piece of toilet paper is stuck to your shoe?

169. What's the proper way to introduce someone?

It's proper to introduce someone who's younger or of less distinction *to* someone who's older or of more distinction. That's because the person who's older or more distinguished may already be known. You'd say, "Mr. President, this is my buddy Larry." You *wouldn't* say, "Larry, this is the president." Larry probably already figured that out.

According to the same rule, you'd introduce your new boyfriend like this: "Mom, this is Ralph." She has a pretty good idea that the guy you're kissing on the doorstep is, in fact, Ralph, but it's best to do it properly. She's less likely to accidentally call him Rick, Raymond, or Rudy—your last three boyfriends.

Another thing. With all the name changes that come with remarriages and blended families, you can't assume that all the last names in one house are the same. If your mom's last name differs from yours, mention her full name when you present someone to her. That tells the person how to address her.

◆

170. Is it okay to call an adult by his or her first name?

The best thing to do is to use the last name until a person *asks* you to use the first name. That way there's no chance of appearing disrespectful.

◆

171. What do you do if you forget someone's name?

The hardest and best thing to do is to admit it. If you do it with humor and grace, the other person won't be offended:

"I'm sorry, but my mind has just gone blank, and I can't recall your name at the moment."

When the person refreshes your memory, repeat the name and then, if possible, say something that shows you may have forgotten the name but not the *person*. Mention something about the last time you met, or inquire about an interest you know you both share.

If you're with another friend when this happens, do what some married couples do for each other. Let's say a wife sees that her husband can't remember a person's name. She steps in and introduces herself. The mystery person introduces himself to her. The husband hears the name and joins the conversation with confidence.

———————— ◆ ————————

172. Your parents taught you to open doors for women, but some people say this is sexist. What's the right thing to do?

Open doors for *everyone*. Being polite isn't a male-to-female thing—it's a person-to-person thing.

———————— ◆ ————————

173. How should you act around a person in a wheelchair?

The same way you act around people NOT in a wheelchair, which means...

Don't lean on the back of the chair. A wheelchair is part of a person's personal space, so leaning on it is like leaning on a person's shoulder.

Sit down. Nobody likes to be talked down to. Whenever possible, sit down and talk eye to eye.

Don't pat. Having one's shoulder and head within easy reach makes the person a target of pats. Nobody likes to be treated like a child or a dog (except children and puppies).

Don't push. Again, the wheelchair is part of a person's space. Help the person only upon request.

— ◆ —

174. How should you act around people who are blind or deaf?

Most people who are blind or deaf can participate in a wide variety of activities. Some people who are blind participate in triathlons; some who are deaf enjoy dancing. Here are some commonsense ways to act.

Blind

- Speak in a normal voice. People often shout when they talk to people who are blind. Remember, someone who is blind can probably hear as well or better than you do.
- Offer assistance only when requested.
- When aiding a blind person, grasp her gently but firmly at the elbow. Walk a half-step ahead. It's not necessary to give constant oral instructions, because she can feel your movements.

Deaf

- If he reads lips, make sure that he can see yours.
- Remember that group conversation jumps around a lot. It may be hard for someone trying to read lips to find who is speaking quickly enough. Help him be part of the conversation.
- If he signs, ask him to teach you rudimentary elements, such as the alphabet and common words, so you can communicate.

— ◆ —

175. How do you know which utensils to use at a multicourse meal?

You're staring at an arsenal of eating utensils and wondering which ones are to be used on what. Here's a simple guide to help you figure it out:

- Work from the outside in. If there are two forks, the outside one is the salad fork.
- Having two knives means one is for salad and one is for the main course. If there's a stubby knife, it's for buttering your bread: park it on the small bread plate in front of your setting. Spoons are easy—the biggest one is for soup.
- When you're finished with a course, put the utensil in the center of the dish. This signal tells the server that you're finished with it so she doesn't have to ask you and interrupt the conversation. (It also prevents the utensil from doing a gainer off the dish and into your lap when the server carries it away.)

◆

176. How do you stop someone from choking?

You probably already know this, but hearing it again doesn't hurt. If someone is choking, you have just four minutes to save the person before the lack of oxygen causes permanent brain damage or death.

The Heimlich Maneuver   First, determine if the person is really choking and not just having a coughing fit. It's possible to hurt someone while trying to help, so be sure to get the go sign before beginning.

1. Quickly stand behind the victim and wrap your arms around the waist.

2. Make a fist and place the thumb side against the victim's abdomen, slightly above the belly button and below the rib cage.

3. Grab your fist with your other hand and give three or four quick, upward thrusts. Note: simply squeezing won't do the trick—you have to use enough force so that air from the lungs dislodges whatever is stuck in the windpipe.

4. If at first you don't succeed, try again—several times if necessary.

Small children and babies require a different procedure that should be learned in a CPR class.

◆

177. Why do guys leave the toilet seat up all the time?

Most times, when a guy uses a toilet, it's like a target. He's just making that target as large as possible.

He leaves the seat up when he's done because there's a good chance that he or some other male will use that toilet next, and putting the seat down would be a complete waste of time and motion. It's a matter of economy.

He has *heard* that girls prefer for him to put the seat down anyway. They don't appreciate sitting down only to discover that there's nothing to prevent them from falling in. But he dismisses their preference because his boyhood was filled with hidden thumbtacks, whoopie cushions, and chairs jerked out from under him. He figures that anyone silly enough to sit without looking first is *destined* for trouble.

◆

178. Why do girls get so mad when guys leave the toilet seat up all the time?

When a girl uses a toilet, it's like a chair. If she sits down when the chair part of it is missing, it's no fun.

◆

179. What should you do when you inhale a fly?

Even with today's more relaxed standards of etiquette, it is considered improper to hurl a fly. The most proper thing to do would be to quietly swallow it and hope no one witnessed the unfortunate event. If someone does see your discomfort and asks what is wrong, cough delicately (you don't want the fly to reappear) and say that you have a bit of phlegm in your throat.

Of course, if the thought of having such a grotesque, germ-bearing creature inside you repulses you so much that you might lose your whole lunch anyway, you must rid yourself of the invading creature. To do so, point in the opposite direction of your cough, shout, "Look—shoe sale!" to your companions, and spit the offending beast into the nearest, most convenient container. Your friend's soft drink cup will do in a pinch.

◆

180. What do you do if you lean against the bathroom counter and get a wet spot on your front?

It happens all the time. Typically, you're on a date. You go into the restroom and lean against the counter to check for midmeal blemishes. The countertop is a fancy marble thing that doesn't show water very well. When you lean back, there's a wet spot on your clothes in the worst possible location. At this point you have three options:

1. If the restroom is equipped with hot-air hand dryers, slip out of your pants or dress and hold them beneath the air stream until dry. If you're very tall, you may be able to do this without taking off your pants—but if you're *that* tall, the wet spot is on your knees anyway.

2. Splash water all over the front of your clothes. When you return to your date, say that the sink exploded.

3. Take off your clothes and soak them in the sink to make them uniformly dark.

◆

181. What do you do when you're in a seat that emits a sound remarkably similar to an actual body noise?

Naugahyde and vinyl seat covers and restaurant booths are notorious for this. The best thing to do is to try to duplicate the noise in a more obvious way by sliding back and forth or by rubbing your hand on the cushion. If these noises only make the situation worse, excuse yourself and run away.

◆

182. Are there any discreet ways to check your zipper?

Grab your belt buckle, running your thumb inside your pants and your index finger to the top of your fly. If your thumb and finger meet unopposed, you've got trouble. To fix the problem, sneeze violently. While you're doubled over, close the zipper.

◆

183. How do you check for body odor without drawing attention to yourself?

Scratch your right shoulder with your left hand and look over your left shoulder at the same time. This will put your nose close to your armpit for an investigative sniff. Repeat with the other arm.

◆

184. What do you do if you're discovered with a portion of your dress tucked into your pantyhose?

Make a fashion statement: tuck in the rest of the dress.

Note: guys can usually avoid this problem by wearing a hoop-skirt.

◆

185. What do you do when people notice that a piece of toilet paper is stuck to your shoe?

Smart people come prepared for just such an occurrence by always carrying a six-foot piece of toilet paper folded in their pocket or purse. Then if someone points to their shoe, they take out the other piece of TP and begin a ballet performance, swirling one piece with one hand while streaming the other with graceful leaps and kicks.

If this embarrassing problem happens to you a lot, stop wearing adhesive-soled shoes into the bathroom.

—— MIND ——

186. What can you do about depression?

Everyone has bad moods. They're no big deal (except for the people around you) because you know they go away after a while.

Depression is a much bigger thing—a feeling of discouragement, an inability to laugh, or hopelessness that can last for weeks, months, or years. Lots of times you can trace the depression to a tragedy such as a death or your parents' divorce. Sometimes you can't figure out the cause—you're just depressed about being depressed.

How you get through your depression depends on how severe it is. Here are some techniques people have used to get beyond it:

Pause   Some people stay so busy they don't stop long enough to figure out why they feel so bad. If you're one of them, take a day off and think about what may be causing the depression. It could be an unresolved conflict with someone you love or a big disappointment you suffered a while ago but haven't gotten over.

Get Some Sun   People in northern climates especially suffer from depression when they've gone too long without sunlight. Sit in a sunny window. If the weather won't let you, study near a special lamp designed to emit sun-like rays.

Exercise   You've probably heard of endorphins, morphine-like substances your body releases into the system in response to stress or exercise. Endorphins make you feel better about yourself and increase your ability to cope with depression. Get your body moving and let the endorphins go to work.

Talk to Someone   Your family and friends have been wondering what's going on inside but haven't known how to help. Now is the time to tell someone what you're feeling. If you don't know why you're depressed, this person may be able to help you figure it out.

Get Help Depression is one of the most common problems therapists and counselors deal with. A professional can help you walk through the dark times so you can get back to enjoying life.

———————— ◆ ————————

187. How do you get rid of a negative attitude?

"Why are you always so negative?" "Quit being negative!" If you've been hearing that a lot lately, you're probably stuck in the "negs"—an unconscious tendency to be sarcastic, use put-downs, and think the worst about things. Unlike multiplication, two negatives don't make a positive: they just make you more negative than ever.

Chronic negative behavior comes from your inside—from anger, pain, or hurt deep inside. When your negs last more than a few hours, it's time to stop and check out the problem. One of the best ways to get over a bout of the negs is *thank therapy*.

Take out a piece of paper and number the lines from one to fifty. Now take several minutes to write down fifty things you're thankful for. Be specific. It's tough at first because the negative thoughts have blocked out most of the good stuff. But after a few minutes you'll get on a roll. If you run out of lines before you run out of things to be thankful for, great! Make more lines and keep going.

When you think you've run out, go back through the list and say thank you to God for each of the things He has allowed you to have. Then fold the paper and carry it around in your pocket for the day. When you catch yourself slipping into the negs again, pull out the list and start thanking.

———————— ◆ ————————

188. How can you break the put-down habit?

Put-downs and sarcastic humor are popular among teenagers. In some friendship circles, they become the primary means of conversing. But even among friends, put-down humor can take its toll. If you're tired of all the ripping, here are two creative ways to break the habit:

Make a No Put-Down Pact   It's tough to stop shooting put-downs if your close friends continue to launch them at you. So call a cease-fire. For one week, no put-downs: no name-calling, no insults, no criticism, no sarcasm. If you get caught in the act, you get punched in the arm.

A few days—and two sore arms—later, you'll feel like a fog has lifted from your friendships. If you're pleased with the results, continue it for another week. This time put-downers pay for their cuts with soft drinks.

Swap Habits   The easiest way to lose a bad habit is to replace it with a good one. The new habit is encouragement. Learning it requires three steps:

Step 1   Read this verse from the Bible: "Finally, brothers, whatever is true, whatever is noble, whatever is right, whatever is pure, whatever is lovely, whatever is admirable—if anything is excellent or praiseworthy—think about such things" (Philippians 4:8).

Step 2   Pick out all the positive words in the verse and write them on an index card or small piece of paper. *True, Noble, Right, Pure, Lovely, Admirable, Excellent, Praiseworthy*. Put the card in your pocket.

Step 3   Every time you're about to talk to someone, pull out the card and review the list. Before you open your mouth, check to be sure the words in your brain are compatible with the words from the list. It's tough work at first, but it gets easier and faster as you "unlearn" the old habit and develop this new one.

◆

189. What's a phobia?

It's an irrational fear that gets in the way of normal living. Let's say you're shaking in your boots because there's a family of black widow spiders crawling into your shorts. This fear *isn't* arachnophobia (fear of spiders) because your fear is *rational*—you have every reason to shake in your boots.

But if you read this example, broke into a cold sweat, started checking your shorts for spiders, and ran for a can of Raid, it's arachnophobia.

Other Irrational Fears

Agoraphobia	fear of open spaces
Acrophobia	fear of heights
Ailurophobia	fear of cats
Aquaphobia	fear of water
Brontophobia	fear of thunder
Claustrophobia	fear of closed spaces
Cynophobia	fear of dogs
Equinophobia	fear of horses
Microphobia	fear of germs
Murophobia	fear of mice
Mysophobia	fear of dirt
Ophidiophobia	fear of snakes
Pyrophobia	fear of fire
Thanatophobia	fear of death
Xenophobia	fear of strangers
Zoophobia	fear of animals

◆

190. What phobias are most common among teenagers?

Orbitophobia	fear of being blown out of your Reebok Pumps by a faulty air valve

Gymnudophobia	fear of getting out of the locker room shower, naked and wet, only to forget your locker combination
Napophobia	fear that you'll awaken to the sound of laughter, look up, then realize that you've fallen asleep in class—leaving a pool of drool on your desk (also known as DTP, or desktop puddling)
Lipophobia	fear that while walking your date to the door to kiss her good night for the first time, you will trip on the curb, step in dog doo, call her by your ex-girlfriend's name, and accidentally lean against the doorbell, causing her parents to come out and see what's the matter

◆

191. What's mental retardation?

It's any condition that prevents the brain from attaining full development, limiting a person's ability to learn and put learning to use. It's measured by IQ. A person with an IQ of 70 or below is considered to be mentally retarded, which includes about 1 percent of the population.

There are four commonly used categories based on IQ. Two people with similar IQs may have very different mental abilities. The categories overlap to allow for these cases.

50–55 to about 70	Mild
35–40 to 50–55	Moderate
20–25 to 35–40	Severe
Below 20–25	Profound

People with mild retardation often live pretty normal lives. People with severe or profound retardation often need to be institutionalized because of the extra care required.

Some people don't know what to do when they meet a person who is mentally retarded. There's no trick to it: use kindness and patience and a smile. Amazingly enough, this very same technique works with elderly people, children, your best friend, people with no legs, stepparents, janitors, teachers, moms, girlfriends, people who can't see, police officers, lab partners, street people, counselors, postal carriers, grandparents, garbage collectors, and even your enemies.

———————— ◆ ————————

192. How do you overcome shyness?

Shyness isn't a bad thing. It's just that outgoing people do most of the talking in this world, and *they* say it is.

If you're shy, that's okay. There's no rule about being able to talk to everyone and anyone wherever you go. But if you feel you're *too* shy at times and want some tips on handling situations, here are a few:

Smile   Shyness is often mistaken for conceit because the shy person feels uncomfortable in a social setting and forgets to smile. People avoid her, which makes her more uncomfortable, which makes her look meaner, which causes people to avoid her even more—it's a downward spiral. But a person who's smiling isn't conceited, she's just quiet.

Listen   Most outgoing people would rather hear the sound of their own voice than the sound of someone else's—and they'll latch onto anyone who shows a genuine interest in hearing it, too. Let the outgoing person do most of the talking at first: when you feel comfortable, jump in.

Play Offense   Some people can't handle being around a shy person—they think it's their sworn duty to "draw you out." They start talking to you like a teacher to a bashful kindergartner. Your only defense from these people is to play offense: take a deep breath and start firing back questions at them. You'll find it's easier to aim the spotlight than it is to stand in it.

Fess Up Let's say you're on a date with someone and you do something stupid like forget your own name or pour ketchup on yourself. Smile and say, "I do dumb things when I'm nervous. And I get nervous around people sometimes because I'm shy." That one line will break more ice than anything an extrovert could do.

——— Money ———

193. How do you save up $500?
194. How can you learn to spend less money?
195. How can you train yourself to save more of your income?
196. Why do banks offer so many different kinds of accounts?
197. Why don't most banks open checking accounts or make loans to teenagers?
198. What's a credit record?
199. How do you fill out a credit application?
200. How do you establish credit?
201. What are mutual funds?
202. How do you make a mutual fund investment if you're under 18?
203. How do stocks work?
204. What's a bond?
205. How do you invest in a CD if you don't have the $500 or $1,000 minimum amount?

193. How do you save up $500?

The first $500 is always the hardest. How long it takes you to get there depends on how much money you make and how well you hold on to what you earn. Here are some tips to get you to the $500 mark:

- If you don't have a regular job, do whatever you can to *make* at least $15.00 per week (only $2.14 each day) for a year. Deposit $10.00 *every* week into a savings account. Use the remaining $5.00 per week as your spending allowance.
- If you have a job, deposit 70 percent of every paycheck in a savings account. If you can get by without junk food every week and new clothes every month, put aside 80 percent. If you're desperate, go for 90 percent.
- Deposit *all* of every birthday check in the account.
- Don't borrow money.
- *Don't make withdrawals from the account* (that's why it's called savings). Money for Christmas gifts and other special expenses should come out of your spending allowance.

◆

194. How can you learn to spend less money?

Most of us don't seem to have any problem spending money; our problem is learning *not* to spend it. Here are some sales "defense" tactics:

- *Ask why.* Ask yourself, "Why do I want to buy this thing?" It's amazing how silly some of your purchases look when you ask that question.
- *Count to seven.* Live by the *seven over seven rule:* anytime you want to buy something that costs over $7, you have to

wait seven days. This will blow a big hole in your impulse buying habits!

• *Don't "save money" by spending it.* Walk away when someone says that a deal is "too good to pass up" or that "you'll never find as good a deal as this one." You will *always* find a better deal. Keeping your money in savings is a better deal. Don't let salespeople pressure you into making decisions "before it's too late." If you shop around, you'll usually find something as good or better—or discover you didn't need the thing after all.

• *Hang around people who spend less.* If the main pastime of your group of friends is shopping, you're probably going to spend more money than you should.

• *Write it down.* Every time you spend money, write down what you bought and how much you paid. Buying something isn't as easy when you have to find your expense book and write down the transaction. Hold a contest with yourself to see how little money you can live on each week. Set goals and reward yourself when you meet them.

• *Get some advisers.* Invite two good friends with smart money habits to be your financial advisers. Whenever you want to spend more than $20 on something, you must present the idea to them and receive their unanimous approval. If they object, you can't buy it.

• *Go on empty.* Each morning put in your wallet only the amount of money you know you'll need for that day's essentials. Keep the extra cash at home.

———————————— ◆ ————————————

195. How can you train yourself to save more of your income?

Instead of buying things that go down in value, save your money and let it work for you.

• *Empty your pockets.* At the end of each day, dump all your pocket change in a jar. Empty the jar every month and deposit the coins in the bank. It seems like a small amount of money, but it adds up over a year into some real cash.

- *Buy off a bad habit.* If you smoke, eat the wrong foods, or drink seven sodas a day, give it up. Figure out how much money you spend on your habit, then put that money in the bank instead.

- *Direct deposit.* Some employers can deposit your paycheck directly into your savings account.

- *Go through withdrawal pains.* If you have a problem keeping your savings in the bank where it belongs, set up an account that requires two signatures for a withdrawal—yours and a parent's.

◆

196. Why do banks offer so many different kinds of accounts?

Banks have lots of fancy names for their different accounts, but most fit into one of four basic categories:

- *Basic Savings* accounts (sometimes called passbook accounts) have little or no minimum balance and pay around 5 percent interest. *Advantages:* You can withdraw your money whenever you want (no minimum deposit period), and you earn more interest than if you hid the money in that secret place near your bed (shh). *Disadvantage:* The interest you earn barely beats inflation in good years and falls way behind in bad ones.

- *Basic Checking* accounts don't pay interest, but they don't cost you anything as long as you keep a minimum balance of $500 to $600. If your balance drops below the minimum, the bank charges you a monthly fee of $5 to $10. Some banks also charge you a few cents per check.

- *Money Market* checking and savings accounts pay better interest than basic savings accounts, with the rate rising according to the amount of the balance. They also have higher minimum balances, usually $1,000 or more. They usually offer ATM (automatic teller machine) cards, which are nice to have if you're shy and don't like talking to human tellers. ATM cards also make night and weekend banking possible for both shy and outgoing customers.

• *Certificates of Deposit* (CDs) are guarantees that you will let the bank keep a certain amount of money (generally $1,000 or more) for a certain period (one month to ten years) in exchange for higher interest. If you withdraw your money before the CD matures, you pay a stiff penalty. Obviously, the more money you give them and the longer they keep it, the more interest they'll guarantee. Some banks offer $500 CDs, which makes them a good investment possibility for lots of teenagers.

◆

197. Why won't most banks open checking accounts or make loans to teenagers?

According to the government, contractual agreements made with minors can't be enforced against you. These laws are designed to protect you from being hurt by bad deals. But they also keep lots of banks and other businesses from entering into legitimate deals with you. For example, if an adult overdraws her checking account by $500 and refuses to pay back the money, the bank can take her to court and make her pay. If you're a minor and do the same thing, the court won't recognize the agreement between you and the bank as a legal contract—the bank loses its money.

This doesn't mean they *can't* do business with you—they just don't have the law to back them up if you go astray. Consequently, most banks won't go very far out of their way to help you. On rare occasions, if your mom or dad is a very good customer of the bank (i.e., keeps loads of money there), they may be willing to let you open a checking or money market account.

More likely, they'll require a parent or guardian to cosign the account. This way they can go after the adult if you go on a spending spree with your checkbook. Many banks tend to be easier on the age restriction with CDs, allowing you to open one without a cosigner. Of course, they're the ones who are holding all your money, so it's no great gesture on their part.

Minor Triumphs   Credit unions are very open to teenage customers. Some offer virtually all the services of a bank, with little of the age discrimination. Some credit unions are open only to employees of a certain company, government office, or industry. A few are open to any worker who wishes to join.

If you're working, you may be able to join a credit union on your own. If your mother or father is a member, the union may also let you join. Because they're non-profit institutions, they're able to offer higher yielding basic savings, money-market, and CD accounts; they can also provide car and personal loans to their members at lower-than-bank interest rates. Many also offer Visa and MasterCard accounts (even to creditworthy seventeen-year-olds).

——————————— ◆ ———————————

198. What's a credit record?

A credit record is your financial reputation. If you want to rent an apartment, buy a house, have a phone hooked up, get a credit card, take out a loan, buy a blimp, or start a business, you need a good record.

A company that wants to check your credit can call other companies that have done money deals with you in the past, or it can get a report from a credit reporting bureau.

——————————— ◆ ———————————

199. How do you fill out a credit application?

Every application is different, but most want this information:

Income   The longer you hold a job, the better you look. Don't lie about your salary or how long you've worked there; they may call your boss to verify the numbers. If you have other sources of income—side jobs, allowance, whatever— be sure to list them, too. Every little bit helps. Save your check stubs. If someone pays you in cash, make out a "bill," mark it paid, and have her sign it. Make sure that the money you earn can be used to prove your ability to earn more of it.

Expenses   You may be asked to list some of your regular expenses such as rent and car insurance. If they don't ask, don't volunteer it; and if they do, list only what is asked for.

Assets   List the amount of money you have in savings and checking accounts (they'll call to verify these, too, so shoot straight). If you have money invested in mutual funds, CDs, stocks, bonds, gold, or pork belly futures, write it down. Be ready to provide the name of the firm that handled these investments for you. These things suggest that you know how to handle your money. You may wish to mention any toys or vehicles you own that are worth several hundred dollars or more: an expensive camera, motorcycle, car, Bell Jet Ranger helicopter.

Liabilities   If you have any debts—auto or personal loans, charge cards—you'll be asked to list your monthly payment and the outstanding balance.

If your monthly expenses all but wipe out your income, they'll figure you don't have enough cushion to make monthly payments on a loan or credit card debt. If your liabilities (what you *owe*) greatly exceed your assets (what you *own*), they don't want to help you dig your grave deeper.

(Actually, they know that once you're *in* the grave, you won't leave enough behind to pay off the debt.)

But if you have a healthy cash flow, low or no debt, and evidence of good money management habits, you're their kind of customer.

◆

200. How do you establish credit?

This is what's called a catch-22. Nobody wants to grant you credit until you have a credit record. But you don't have a credit record until you make regular payments on a credit account. Actually, it's not as bad as it seems. The trick is to start small.

1. If you're eighteen or older, apply for a credit card from Sears, Montgomery Ward, or another large department store. These are typically the easiest to qualify for.

2. When you get the card, use it to make one small purchase each month for six months. Make sure it's something you would have bought that month anyway, or charge something your parents need and have them reimburse you for it.

3. Pay your balance in full the moment you get the bill. If you bounce a check or make a late payment, you'll defeat your purpose. By paying the balance in full, you avoid paying interest on the "loan," which wastes your money.

4. Each month your payment record is sent to the credit bureau. It will begin a credit record on you, which will be spotless due to your outstanding payment habits.

5. Apply for your next charge card. If your application is accepted, you may wish to close your first card's account by cutting the card in half.

◆

201. What are mutual funds?

Here's your chance to own stock in dozens of companies. A mutual fund is a collection of stocks, bonds, or other kinds of investments bought by a bunch of people and managed by professionals. It's kind of like a club: everyone who puts money in the fund owns portions of every investment in the fund.

Let's say you have $500 to invest. You could buy 100 shares of a stock trading at $5 per share, but that's putting all your eggs in one basket. You could spread things around by buying 20 shares in five different companies, but the stockbroker would charge you about *$200* to buy them for you.

If you pooled your money with nine other people with $500 each, your group would have a fund with $5,000 to invest. Then you could buy several stocks and spread the risks and costs among you. Your share is 10 percent of every stock owned by the group: if one company doesn't do well, the performance of the others can offset the loss. That is how a mutual fund works.

With a mutual fund, thousands of people invest varying amounts, and professional managers choose which investments will be best for everyone in the group. Since the fund manager often has millions of dollars to work with, he usually invests in fifty to one hundred different securities (stocks, bonds, etc.).

————————— ◆ —————————

202. How do you make a mutual fund investment if you're under 18?

Nearly all mutual funds are sold directly by the investment companies and financial institutions that manage them. But before accepting your money, a fund is required to send you a *prospectus*—a report describing the fund's investment goals, risks, trading procedures, and past performance. If you do decide to buy shares in a fund, you'll have to send a check for at least the minimum amount, typically $250 to $1,000. After that, you can usually make additional investments of $250 or more, as often as you like.

You need to be 18 to invest in a mutual fund by yourself. If not, you can ask an adult to buy the shares for you as a gift under the Uniform Gift to Minors Act (UGMA). The investment is yours, but your trustee (the adult) is legally responsible for the transactions. The fund office will tell you how to do this.

If you're buying a *load* fund, you'll also have to pay a commission to the fund manager—from 3 to 8.5 percent, depending on the fund. There's generally no charge when you sell. (Okay, just to be different, some load funds charge an exit fee when you sell, but nothing when you buy. A few get you at both ends.) A *no-load* fund won't charge you a sales fee. Some funds have limits or penalties if you sell your shares back to them too quickly; the prospectus describes these and other fees.

Like many legal documents, prospectuses are not always easy to understand. A good source of mutual fund information is *Money* magazine, which tracks the best performing funds each month in a variety of categories. They also tell you how various funds have done over the past year and five years. Their listings also include toll-free numbers and you can call to receive prospectuses. Annually, *Money, Business Week,* and other magazines print ratings for all major mutual funds to help you compare funds and learn about their managers' strategies.

Many funds perform well only during certain stages of an economic cycle; a fund that's hot at the beginning of a period of economic good times may lose all its sizzle—and some of your money—in the middle of the party. Some funds are so temperamental that you'll see them at the top of the performance list one month and at the bottom the next. It's important to consider a fund's one and five-year track record. *All-weather* funds tend to survive the ups and downs better. They may not have killer performance records each month, or even for the past year, but their five-year record is impressive.

◆

203. How do stocks work?

When you own a share of stock, you own a portion of the company. If the company does well and the stock value goes up, you can sell your share for a *capital gain*. If the company has healthy profits, it may set aside a portion to send to each shareholder in the form of a *dividend*. These are the two main ways of making money with stock.

To buy stock, you have to use a middleman called a stockbroker, who charges you a commission for his work. The minimum commission (for the smallest orders) is about $40 or more; if you buy $500 worth of stock in one company, you have to earn 8 percent on the investment just to cover the commission.

When you sell it, you'll pay another $40. That means your stock has to rise in value by 16 percent or pay huge dividends just for you to break even! You can see that small investments in stock are really expensive. Stock mutual funds are a better deal for smaller investors.

---◆---

204. What's a bond?

Bonds are loans to companies and governments. With most bonds, you lend the issuer $1,000 for a certain time period —up to thirty years. You receive interest every year, and you get the $1,000 back at the end of the loan.

Bonds are good for people who need to earn a regular income from their investments to cover expenses. But you already have income from an allowance or part-time job, so you're better off with investments that grow bigger—growth funds and certificates of deposit. *Zero coupon bonds* grow bigger over time. Instead of paying you the interest each year, they pay it all at once at the end of the loan. Some people use "zeros" to save for college. They buy one bond that matures (pays off) at the beginning of their freshman year, another that matures at the start of their sophomore year, and so on. The money becomes available precisely when they need it most.

———————— ◆ ————————

205. How do you invest in a CD if you don't have the $500 or $1,000 minimum amount?

Here are three ways to come up with the minimum:

- *Sweating*. It's really tough to make an investment return that outpaces inflation if you don't have this kind of money. Save your allowance, store up the birthday checks, work a few extra hours—and above all, *spend less*.
- *Pooling*. You're not the only one with this problem. Find one or two friends with some money to invest. Put in identical amounts and set up the account so that each of you has to sign for the money. At the end of the period divide the principal (the original investment amount) and interest evenly. (This is just a smaller version of a mutual fund.)
- *Bumping*. Hang out in front of the bank. If a rich old lady walks out carrying a handful of cash, accidentally bump into her and see if she drops it. Just kidding—bumping is like pooling, except you're just using someone else's money to bump you into the "big leagues." A relative with money in the bank may be willing to let you use a few hundred dollars of it for a bump if you agree to pay her the portion of the interest that's hers. For example, if she puts in $700 to bump your $300, pay her 70 percent of the yield. Keep track of her money and repay it when your savings can stand on their own.

If you're investing in CDs, it's best to track the direction of interest rates each week or so. If interest rates are on the rise, invest in CDs with terms of one to six months. The faster they rise, the shorter the term you should select. You don't want to lock your money up at a lower rate when you could be getting better interest soon. The opposite is also true. If interest rates are falling (and you think they'll continue to do so), lock in a high rate for a year or two.

It's also good to compare your bank's CD rate with other banks in your area just to make sure they're paying you a competitive rate. If not, go elsewhere. Each month, *Money* magazine lists the top-yielding CDs and money market accounts in the country, as well as the national averages. You can instantly see how well (or poorly) you're doing. The listing even includes the top-paying banks' phone numbers, which you can call to request an application. Oftentimes you can open an account simply by mailing a check with the signed application.

When a CD matures, you've got to decide what to do with the money: invest in another CD, deposit the money in a savings account, or take it out of the bank. Make your decision before the CD matures so the money doesn't sit around, earning zero interest while you make up your mind.

──Planet──

206. What can you do to stop world hunger?

Here   You can help feed hungry people in your community with some of the ideas listed in the answer to question 212.

There   One of the most effective ways to make a long-term difference in lives of hungry people is to join a child sponsorship program. Organizations such as Compassion International and World Vision can link you with a kid in another part of the planet who needs help to survive. For about $20 a month you can help provide food, a home, and an education. Most programs let you write letters back and forth and keep you informed on your child's progress.

Some people feel that child sponsorship programs are inadequate because they favor one kid to the exclusion of the rest of the kids in a village. In practice, it doesn't work out that way. Here's why:

- Some of your money goes to the child's family, so all the children benefit (Third World families tend to be large).
- Some of your money goes to the kid's school, which uses it to hire and train teachers, buy books and equipment, and deliver a better education to all its students.
- Some of your money may go to a church or community agency in the village to pay for a well, water purification system, farm equipment, or medical facility.
- Some of your money goes to the organization's field office, which helps other families and advises community leaders in farming, conservation, economic development, and public health.
- Most of all, your money provides hope and vision and purpose to a child who will grow up to become a leader in her community and country. In the end it's not money or programs that transform countries—it's people. Your sponsored child will be one of those people.

If you'd like to sponsor a child, contact one of these organizations:

Compassion International
P.O. Box 7000
3955 Cragwood Dr.
Colorado Springs, CO 80933
1-800-336-7676

World Vision
Childcare Sponsorship
Pasadena, CA 91131
1-800-777-5777

◆

207. Why can't countries manage their money and food to prevent famines?

There are two basic reasons:

They Can't Grow Enough Food   Much of the land in the U.S. is good for growing food. We have good soil, ample rainfall, and lots of trucks and trains and boats to get the food from the farms to where people live. In fact, we have *too much* farmland—we can grow more food than we can swallow.

Most of the rest of the world has the opposite problem. There's not enough good soil or water or means to move the food around. To make up the difference, they've got to figure out ways to grow and transport food more efficiently (which takes money), or they have to buy their food from someone else (more money). Which explains the other reason...

They Don't Have Enough Money   They get their money by selling stuff to other countries—oil, coffee, minerals, cheap labor, whatever they've got. But if they don't have much to sell, or if the cost of transporting the stuff to countries that want it is too high, they run out of money before they run out of needs.

Even if they manage to squeak by from year to year, they can't handle a disaster such as a drought. There are no food reserves and no money set aside for emergencies.

◆

208. How do you jump start a Third World country?

Here are some of the most popular ways:

Imports Buying products made in that country usually puts money in the pockets of those who made them.

Foreign Investment Here's how it works. An international company may decide it's a good idea to open a factory or run a business in that country to take advantage of local resources, inexpensive labor, or some other benefit. The company builds a factory and hires local citizens. These workers spend their paychecks on food and furniture and houses, which means employment for store owners and furniture makers and house builders, who use *their* money to open more stores, expand furniture factories, and build more houses.

The sales and income tax on all this money helps the government build roads, phone systems, water projects, hospitals, and schools—which entices more companies to do business there. Or something like that.

Loans Banks sometimes lend money to governments to help them do some of this on their own. They figure that the countries can pay them back when the economy improves.

Financial Aid Sometimes governments, corporations, and private foundations give money to a country or its people to fund food, education, and development projects. You can do this yourself through a child sponsorship program (see question 202).

Education Teachers, missionaries, and business and technical experts from other countries train people to improve their own country. You can do this by becoming a missionary or a Peace Corps volunteer.

◆

209. How can you get your family to start recycling?

People who don't recycle have two excuses: it's too much hassle, or they don't know how. Here's what you can do to change things at your house:

- Get excited. If you are, your family eventually will be, too.
- Find a place in the house where recyclables can be stored (you may have to clean out the garage, a closet, or a corner of the porch).
- Make or buy bins for recycled materials. (Some communities provide these to residents.) Be sure to have bins for aluminum cans, glass containers, plastic bottles, and newspapers. Depending on the recycling available in your area, you also may want to provide bins for colored glass, regular paper, and cardboard.
- Be the bin captain. Make sure the bins get emptied regularly, either at a recycling center or, if it's available, at the curb.
- Buy food and household supplies in bulk.
- Buy stuff that is packaged efficiently to cut down waste.
- Take your own bags to the market. Use canvas shopping bags, or reuse the paper or plastic ones they gave you last time.
- If you have a yard, create a compost heap. Feed it yard cuttings and table scraps (just about anything but meat— it's a vegetarian).

◆

210. Why do people become vegetarians?

People become vegetarians for all sorts of reasons. They also define vegetarianism differently. Here are the major vegetarian classifications:

Lacto-ovo vegetarians don't eat meat but do eat dairy products (*lacto*) and eggs (*ovo*). Some lacto-ovos, called *lacto-ovo-pescas*, also eat fish.

Strict vegetarians, also known as *vegans,* abstain from eating all animal products. Most also avoid buying leather products or anything else that came from an animal; if tests on animals were used to develop or test the product, most vegans will avoid the product.

These classifications usually relate to the reasons a person becomes a vegetarian. Of course there are exceptions, but most lacto-ovos become so for health, economic, ecological, or world hunger reasons. Vegans often cite animal rights or spiritual reasons.

Here are some of those reasons explained:

Animal Rights   Some people are disgusted with what they feel are cruel farming practices such as overcrowding, force-feeding, and excessive use of drugs and hormones. Others believe *any* use of an animal in farming is cruel.

Ecology and World Hunger   To produce one pound of meat protein, a cow must be fed at least sixteen pounds of mostly consumable grain.[1] Many people feel this is a terrible waste of resources—especially when one of those resources, grain, could be used to feed hungry people instead of cattle.

Economics   Meat is expensive. Other protein alternatives cost less.

Nutrition   Red meat contains a lot of fat and cholesterol. Most people who cut down or eliminate red meat from their diets say they feel better and have more energy.

Spiritual   Some religions such as Hinduism encourage the practice of vegetarianism.

◆

211. Is vegetarianism a safe option for you?

It can be if you're smart. You do need protein, especially if you are still growing. However, meat is not the end-all of protein resources. Vegetarian alternatives yield the amino acids that make complete proteins. If you are serious about vegetarianism, be serious about the way you become one. Pick up a vegetarian cookbook that also explains how the protein thing works. Look for the following titles:

- *Laurel's Kitchen* (New York: Bantam Books, 1976)
- *Diet for a Small Planet* (New York: Ballantine, 1971)
- *Recipes for a Small Planet* (New York: Ballantine, 1973)

◆

212. How long does it take a hot dog to decompose in a landfill?

It depends on the hot dog and what you put on it (relish acts as a preservative). But if you bury a plain hot dog in a landfill, it takes about forty years.

◆

213. What's the greenhouse effect?

Greenhouses let in the sun's rays—both visible and ultraviolet light. When these light waves hit objects inside the greenhouse, they warm them. These heated objects warm the air that's trapped inside by the glass roof and walls.

Our planet can behave the same way. The sun heats up the earth, which radiates heat into the air that's trapped by a "roof"—gravity's grip on our atmosphere. The more "stuff" floating in the atmosphere, the less leaky the roof (which is why cloudy nights are warmer than clear ones).

This greenhouse thing is normally a good deal—it keeps the planet warm. The problem arises when the atmosphere gets too good at retaining the heat. That can happen from...

...too much carbon dioxide. This gas is a major insulation blanket, keeping the planet 54°F warmer than it would be without it. The burning of fossil fuels creates a lot of carbon dioxide. Cutting down trees that process CO_2 doesn't help, either.

...too much air pollution. Dust in the air acts as insulation, too. You'd think it would just block the sunlight from getting through in the first place, but much of the ultraviolet light sneaks in anyway (you figure this out on your own the first time you get sunburned on a cloudy day).

...not enough ozone. This gas forms a giant sunblock around the planet, preventing much of the ultraviolet from getting through. Certain pollutants, such as the stuff used in car air conditioners, destroy the ozone. Using the greenhouse analogy, this is like cleaning the windows so more light gets in. (Ozone also protects us from skin cancer, which can be caused by ultraviolet light.)

The fear is that these factors will raise the temperature of the whole planet by a few degrees, altering weather patterns and melting the ice at the poles—which raises the ocean levels (which will mess up several really good surf spots).

Some experts dispute the global warming theory because, despite the recent increases in air pollution, carbon dioxide production, deforestation, and ozone destruction, a rise in global temperatures hasn't been proven decisively. In other words, in a few years this answer will be either prophetic or silly.

However, each of these things—air pollution, ozone destruction, etc.—is bad all by itself, regardless of what it does to the temperature. We need to act now to save our planet.

◆

214. Can you do anything about global warming?

Yes! It's easy.

Plant Trees *eat* carbon dioxide and spit out oxygen (so to speak). Plant a tree or two in your yard this week.

Bike It's not the vehicle of choice among those who've finally obtained their license to burn gasoline, but it really does makes a difference. Car exhaust, gas fumes, and dust from tire treads help form the roof of the global greenhouse. Bikes don't. Besides, you can't do a wheelie with a car.

Give Organizations such as Global Releaf and Floresta use your contributions to plant new forests and prevent the unnecessary mowing down of old ones.

Global Releaf	American Forestry Association P.O. Box 2000, Dept. GR2 Washington, DC 20013
Floresta	1015 Chestnut Ave., F-2 Carlsbad, CA 92008-2562 619-434-6311

◆

215. Why don't street people just get jobs?

Because...

...Most are teenage runaways or children of parents without homes.

...Many are mentally ill. They once lived in mental health facilities. They had to leave when the government cut the amount of money it gave to support these institutions.

...Some are drug addicts whose addiction has taken over their lives.

...A few (very few) are just plain lazy and don't mind living in a cardboard box.

...Some are homeless because they lost their jobs, got into debt, couldn't pay the rent, got kicked out of their apartments, had no family or friends to help them, and had nowhere else to go.

These people *are* looking for jobs, but it's not easy when you're on the street. They have to apply and interview for jobs unbathed (showers are pretty scarce in public restrooms), wearing wrinkled clothes (nowhere to plug in the iron they don't own). They have no address to put on the application and no phone number the employer can call to say, "You're hired" (it's hard to hook a message machine to a pay phone).

The good news is that you can help these people get jobs by giving money to a rescue mission or homeless shelter. Your money can pay for counseling, job training, interview coaching; it may even be used to buy an iron for straightening wrinkled collars. Call the Salvation Army and other organizations in your area to find out how they can invest your money.

———————— ◆ ————————

216. How can you help the homeless?

Here are ten ways:

1. Search your house for extra blankets or coats that can be given away. Take them to a shelter tonight.
2. Volunteer at a shelter or food kitchen. Many churches have such facilities. You'll cook 20 gallons of chicken soup or serve 97 plates of spaghetti or wash 247 dirty dishes.
3. Ask your club or youth group to sponsor a homeless

family. Your group comes up with an apartment and provides food until they can get a place of their own.

4. Carry a small jar of peanut butter in your car or backpack. If someone asks you for money, give him the peanut butter instead—it's full of protein and easy to eat.

5. Get a group of friends together and make sack lunches from the leftovers in your refrigerators. Hand them out downtown.

6. If you see a needy person on your way into a fast-food restaurant, buy an extra burger and give it to her.

7. Give your aluminum cans and other recyclables to collectors.

8. Start a conversation. Just a smile and a kind word can light up someone's day.

9. If you see someone outside the supermarket with a WILL WORK FOR FOOD sign, ask your folks to "hire" him. Here's someone who won't mind helping you clean out the garage, paint the porch, or do the yard work. Feed him lunch and send him away with a generous supply of packaged food from your pantry.

10. Give money each month to an organization serving the homeless in your area. Visit the project to make sure you're making a wise investment.*

◆

217. How do you know if you're giving money to a legitimate cause?

Some people will give money to *anything*. To test this theory, a journalist set up a charity called The Fund for the Widow of the Unknown Soldier (think about it). People gave.[2]

Anyone can start a charitable organization. All you need is a

*For more ideas, pick up *52 Ways to Help Homeless People* by Gary Temple, Jr. (no relation to this author) (Nashville: Oliver-Nelson, 1991).

cause, some friends to serve on a "board of directors," and a few legal documents. There's no law that says most of the money has to go toward the cause: some organizations spend almost all the donations to pay salaries and expenses for soliciting donations. What's worse, some organizations aren't even nonprofit—they collect money and give nothing to the cause they say they support.

Here are a few ways to ensure that your money is going where you think it is:

- Don't pledge money over the phone unless you're familiar with the organization—and can prove that the person you're speaking to truly represents it. (Bogus outfits often have names that sound a whole lot like well-known ones.)

- Don't use 900 numbers to give: about half the money charged to your bill goes to the phone company and the company that processes the calls.

- Be sure the group has a realistic goal.

- Give with your heart but use your head: organizations should be able to supply more than emotional appeal. Get the facts.

- Find out what percentage of every dollar ends up going to the people or place they claim. The costs of running an organization (office, staff, advertising, etc.) vary from one cause to the next but should generally be no more than forty cents of each dollar.

- Ask to see their tax statement—nonprofits must make it available to anyone who asks.

- Consider volunteering. You can get a firsthand look at where your money is going.

- If you suspect a scam, call the police. The next person they call on may not be as cautious.

──── SEX ────

218. How can you make sex "safe"?
219. What are the most overworked lines people use to persuade someone to have sex?
220. What do you say to someone who is pressuring you to have sex?
221. How can you tell if you have a sexually transmitted disease?
222. Why do some people choose abstinence?
223. Why are flesh magazines targeted at men?

218. How can you make sex "safe"?

You can't.

That's one of the great things about sex—it's wild and thrilling and dangerous. Sex is as much emotional and spiritual as it is physical. Putting a condom between you and your partner protects you only physically: there are no condoms to fit your heart and soul.

You *can't* make sex harmless. But you *can* make it less dangerous.

Physical Safety AIDS, sexually transmitted diseases (STDs), pregnancy—sex can sure mess up your health. Here's what you can do to keep your body safe:

Abstain. It's the only foolproof method for protecting your body. And it's still the number one choice among most teenagers (despite what you read).

Choose monogamy. For the benefit of the handful of people left in this world who haven't heard this: when you have sex with someone, you're having sex with everyone that person has ever had sex with. It's a perverse game of tag: Gayle tags Greg, Greg tags Gidget, Gidget tags Gary (and Gil and Garth and Gomez). Sex is safer when it's one-on-one.

Use a condom. You get HIV (the AIDS virus) from infected blood or semen. If your infected partner's blood or semen gets into your bloodstream (usually through the very small tears in sex organ tissue that occur from the rigors of sex), you're exposed. Oral sex is risky, too: your mouth has tiny sores that can provide the virus with a gateway to your bloodstream. By the way, other STDs don't even need to get into your blood. Some can make the "jump" merely by touching body parts.

Emotional and Spiritual Safety As one authority (God) put it, when two people have sex, they become "one flesh." Most of us have a tough enough job keeping our own lives in order. Taking on another heart—and giving away our own—isn't a casual thing. And it's certainly not safe.

Which is why monogamy, aka marriage, has been such a popular idea over the centuries. Here's how it works: (1) find someone you can trust with your entire being, and who can trust you with the same; (2) promise to give yourselves to each other exclusively; and (3) keep your promise.

Sex in this setting is still wild and thrilling...yet safe for heart and soul.

———————— ◆ ————————

219. What are the most overworked lines people use to persuade someone to have sex?

- "All our friends are doing it."
- "We won't go all the way."
- "I've never met a woman (or man) like you before."
- "I will show you how to do it."
- "I want to marry you, so why not?"
- "No one has ever cared for me like you do."
- "Prove you love me."
- "I'll still respect you."
- "Trust me. I know what I'm doing."
- "But I love you!"
- "No one will know."
- "Don't you love me?"
- "But it feels so right."
- "You don't know what you're missing!"
- "You can't get pregnant the first time."
- "You can't get pregnant this time of the month."
- "It will bring us closer together."
- "I can't stop myself."
- "Don't be selfish."
- "If not now, when?"

———————— ◆ ————————

220. What do you say to someone who is pressuring you to have sex?

- "I have principles, you know. I'm against anything that causes the windows to steam up."
- "If we go any further, a strange thing will happen to me. I'll feel guilty. And when I feel guilty, I become miserable, and then I make others miserable. Let's stop here while we both feel good."
- "We'd better stop here. Last time a guy got this close to me, my father shot him and had him mounted in the den. And I didn't even think he was that good-looking."
- "I'm horrible at decisions when I'm breathing hard—let's talk about it later."
- "A while ago I made some decisions on what was right for me in a relationship, and I decided to draw a line at this point. Excuse me while I get a marking pen."
- "No."

———————◆———————

221. How can you tell if you have a sexually transmitted disease?

About two-thirds of all sexually transmitted disease (STD) cases occur among people under twenty-five. Common warning signs include...

- a sore anywhere on the genitals.
- burning or itching during urination.
- unusual genital pain.
- discharge from vagina or penis.

It's easier to detect a problem in males. For example, four out of five women infected with gonorrhea or chlamydia show no symptoms and find out only from a lab test. STDs are extremely virile if untreated. In other words, they don't go away on their own, and they spread easily to anyone you have sex with.

If you think you may have a problem, see a physician immediately.

———————— ◆ ————————

222. Why do some people choose abstinence?

Most teenagers abstain from sexual intercourse. They do so for all sorts of reasons. Here are a few:

- It's the only method of birth control that's 100 percent effective.
- It's the only form of birth control that's free of all side effects.
- It reduces the risk of getting sexually transmitted diseases.
- Abstinence reduces the threat of cervical cancer in women, which increases with early sexual activity and multiple partners.
- It reduces the risk of getting AIDS.
- A couple may find that delaying sex focuses attention on other important areas of a relationship.
- Abstinence can be a test of love.
- Abstinence can make people better lovers because it forces them to explore less physical means of expressing love.

———————— ◆ ————————

223. Why are flesh magazines targeted at men?

Men tend to be stimulated by visual cues more than women are. Women tend to be stimulated more by verbal cues—romance novels and sex articles in women's magazines.

VIOLENCE

224. Are teenagers becoming more violent?

Yes. One measurement of violent tendencies is the amount of teenagers who carry weapons. In 1990, the Centers for Disease Control conducted a survey of nearly 12,000 students across the country. The results were stunning. Nearly 1 in 5 high-school students had carried a weapon in the past 30 days.

Of those who admitted to carrying a weapon, 55 percent carried a knife or sharp instrument, 24 percent carried a club, and 21 percent carried a gun.[1]

———————— ◆ ————————

225. Does watching violence on television and film make you more violent?

This question has been debated for decades. Lots of social scientists have conducted studies to determine the answer. To date, these experiments haven't conclusively proven or disproven the theory.

Most of these studies have focused on the short-term effects of media violence on children. A typical study might show an aggressive television show to one classroom of kids and a prosocial show to a second classroom of children, then observe their behaviors on the playground thirty minutes later. If the first group had tied all the kids in the second classroom to the monkey bars with jump ropes, the theory was proven.

Although kids exposed to aggressive media sometimes copied the behavior on the playground, the results weren't so obvious that one could say the case was closed.

But the problem with these kinds of experiments is that they fail to measure the *cumulative* effects of long-term exposure to violence on television. Between your sixth and nineteenth birthdays, you will view eighteen thousand murders on television. Roughly 80 percent of the shows on television contain aggressive behavior.[2]

How does this outrageous overexposure to violence affect you? Does it alter your views on violence? Does it increase your acceptance of aggressive behavior in others? Does it make you blind to the violence around you?

Filmmaker and youth worker Jim Hancock sums it up with this question to teenagers: "Do you think you can watch fifty thousand violent acts on the screen and not be affected? If you can, is that good news?"[3]

◆

226. What happens when you get shot with a gun?

Most of us have seen thousands of people get shot on television and in movies. But these media haven't done a good job of showing us what it's really like to be hit with a bullet from a gun. Here are the facts:

Fact 1: There's no safe place to get hit by a bullet
We've seen plenty of shows in which the hero gets shot in the arm or leg and keeps on fighting. Not quite. If a bullet goes through your leg, the *best* thing you can hope for is that it passes clean through, leaving holes in both sides and a mean path in between, piercing your flesh, fat, and muscle. The pain from that alone can stop you cold.

Fact 2: Bullets seldom go clean through
There aren't a lot of straight paths in your body. Arteries, organs, nerves, and bones hang in the way. If the bullet severs a major artery, you'll be dead before the ambulance is halfway to the scene. If it severs a nerve, you may lose feeling forever, or you may become paralyzed. And if the bullet hits a bone, the bone or the bullet may fragment—break into little bits—each

piece becoming a mini-projectile for severing arteries, organs, and nerves.

Fact 3: Bullets fight dirty Even the goriest films don't show the dirty tricks bullets play on the human body: people who can't talk (bullet in the throat), can't see (shot in the eyes), can't walk (bullet through the spinal cord), can't control their bladders or can't have sex (shot in the groin). Bullets don't care what they hit or how much damage they do.

◆

227. What can you do to keep from being raped?

You don't have to live in fear or rearrange your whole lifestyle to avoid becoming a rape victim. Here are some simple precautions:

On the Street
- Don't venture out alone in areas with poor lighting—especially where trouble occurs frequently.
- Keep toward the edge of the curb, where you are visible.
- If you suspect that someone is following you, leave the curb and walk in the middle of the street with the cars.
- If you think you may be attacked, run in the road and scream.

By the Car
- Park by a street lamp.
- Never leave your car unlocked.
- Check the backseat and under the car before getting in.

At Home

• Keep locks on doors and windows.
• Install a peephole in the front door.
• Ask for an ID before opening the door to any stranger.

It's always a good idea to take a self-defense course, whether you're fearful of rape or not. Most courses teach psychological handling as well as physical prevention.

◆

228. What do you do if you *are* raped?

Most women who've been raped never report the crime. They stay quiet out of fear, embarrassment, guilt, or because they don't want to recount the experience to police and in a courtroom. Yet those who report the crime often feel a sense of triumph and vindication that cannot come when the crime is kept secret.

If you've been raped, here's what's best to do:

• Contact a family member or trusted friend who can support you through this ordeal.
• Report the crime to the police. If you cannot, have your friend do so.
• Contact your doctor and ask for an immediate visit.
• If your doctor isn't available, go to the nearest emergency room.
• Do not take a shower or bath. This is most women's immediate reaction, but it damages evidence that will help put the rapist away.
• Take off the clothing you were wearing, but don't wash it. Put it in a bag for doctors and police to examine (more critical evidence).
• Try to remember details about the person who assaulted you. Keep a notepad by you and write down things you

remember: voice tone and accent, words used, smell—whatever you can recall.

- Don't stay at home alone. Ask a friend or family member to stay with you.
- Contact the nearest rape crisis center for support and counseling.

If all this seems too much, don't get stressed out about it: just look in the phone book for the number of the child abuse hotline (if you're a minor) or rape crisis center. The folks at these numbers will walk you through the process.

229. What do you do when your car won't start?
230. Why do cockroaches seem to survive everything we do to destroy them?
231. Why do they make sequels to really bad movies?
232. Why do sinks have that little S-shaped pipe at the bottom?
233. Why don't road maps ever fold up right?
234. Where would we be without toilets?
235. Who's been sleeping in my bed?
236. How many pickled peppers did Peter Piper pick?
237. Does anyone have the same Social Security number *and* nine-digit zip code?
238. Why are manhole covers round?
239. How does soap make things clean?
240. How do those little spokes on a bicycle wheel hold all that weight?
241. What happens when you drive away with the gas nozzle still attached to your car?
242. If *October* means "eighth month," how come it's the tenth month of the year?
243. Why do some months have 30 days and others have 31?
244. How come Easter is celebrated sometimes in March and sometimes in April?
245. What are the chances of being born on a leap day?
246. How do magicians saw people in half?
247. What's the big deal about caviar?
248. How do they get lead in pencils?
249. How do movies get rated?
250. How do they pick the pope?
251. How come little kids ask so many questions?
252. What are the plastic things on six-packs called?

253. Why do you need to check the oil when the engine is warm?
254. Why aren't magazines arranged so that you can read an uninterrupted article?
255. Why does Ivory soap float?
256. How does a polygraph machine work?
257. How do rock climbers stick to cliffs?
258. What should you do if your car begins to overheat?
259. What does it take to rent an apartment?

229. What do you do when your car won't start?

If the Key Won't Even Turn Inside the Ignition Switch...

- Check to see that you've got the right key!
- Wiggle the steering wheel around to release the locking mechanism.
- Wiggle the key inside the slot—a worn or bent key may take some coaxing to fit.

The Key Turns, but You Don't Hear the Sound of the Starter Motor...

- Check the gearshift lever—cars with automatic transmissions start only in park or neutral.
- Check the clutch—some cars with manual transmissions won't start unless your foot is on the clutch.
- Check the headlight switch—if the headlights or any other lights were left on, you probably have a dead battery.

The Starter Motor Runs, but the Engine Doesn't Kick in...

- Check the fuel—you may be out of gas (or the fuel line may be blocked or frozen, or you may be low on fuel and parked on a hill).
- Check the spark plug wires to see that they're connected from the ignition to the spark plugs—a "friend" may be playing a trick on you by loosening the wires. (Don't touch the ends while someone is trying to start the car— the shock is unforgettable.)
- Call a friend, mechanic, or tow truck.

———— ◆ ————

230. Why do cockroaches seem to survive everything we do to destroy them?

Roaches are the ultimate survival machine. They can withstand zaps of radiation that would kill any human. They can go without water for three weeks. Two dozen roaches can live off the glue of one stamp for a week. And if they run out of food entirely, they eat each other.

Worst of all, they multiply like...roaches. At the end of one year a single pair of cockroaches can boast of having one hundred thousand offspring. You'll never meet most of them: for every cockroach you see, there are probably two hundred to one thousand hiding somewhere you can't get to.[1]

◆

231. Why do they make sequels to really bad movies?

- Because they want to redeem themselves.
- Because people less discerning than you are thought the first one was pretty good.
- Because people who never heard of *Pets That Bite* will see the ad for *Pets That Bite 2* and say, "Let's go rent the first one! It MUST have been good enough to have a sequel."

◆

232. Why do sinks have that little S-shaped pipe at the bottom?

It's your protection from the sewer. If the sink drained straight into the pipe going into the sewer, the same pipe would act as an air vent when there was no liquid running through the pipe. That would treat your home to all sorts of odors hanging out in sewers.

The S-shaped pipe is actually called a trap because it traps a little bit of water at the bottom of the S, which seals off the sink from sewer gases. Where do these gases go instead? Up and out of those stubby little smokestack pipes on your roof.

If your sink does smell, the trap itself may be filled with gunk and grease and hair. You can clean it out with a chemical drain cleaner or a flexible "pipe snake." Or you can remove the pipe and clean it by hand.

Toilets also have a trap—the toilet itself. The water sitting in the bottom of a toilet seals off the pipe going out of the toilet (you can see the passage in the bottom of the toilet rising as it makes it past the bowl). There's no valve back there that opens up when you flush.

The toilet "flushes" when the weight of the water being poured into the bowl from the tank is great enough to push through the S-curve in the bottom of the toilet. To test this theory, try flushing the toilet with a bucket of water. You can't put too much water into the bowl (unless something is stuck in the pipe) because the weight of the water eventually overwhelms the trap.

◆

233. Why don't road maps ever fold up right?

It's not the map's problem. Maps actually fold perfectly and logically, unlike a newspaper or a fitted sheet. The problem is the mood you're in when you try to fold it: you're lost, you're tired, and you feel like an idiot because you've had to give in and look at a big dumb picture of a bunch of roads. The only intelligent response is to take it out on the map.

So just get it over with: bend the vertical folds *horizontally* (OUCH!), fold the horizontals *backward* (YEOW!), crumple the whole thing into a ball (OOF!), and cram it back in the glove compartment.

◆

234. Where would we be without toilets?

Probably out in some cold smelly outhouse. Flush toilets were invented about four hundred years ago. Installing one in a home meant piping water into a small room, which became the *water closet*—a term still used in some places.

It was invented by a godson of Queen Elizabeth I, Sir John Harington. Notice the similarity between the knight's first name and a popular slang term for bathroom. By the way, he also recommended that it be flushed once or twice per day.

———————— ◆ ————————

235. Who's been sleeping in my bed?

Of course you recognize the question. Members of the bear family asked it prior to their altercation with the burglar Goldilocks. The problem with a question like this is that it just raises more questions. Can bears talk? Do they sleep in beds?

Most important, if they're capable of inquiring, "Who's been eating my porridge?" and "Who's been sitting in my chair?" don't you think they'd be asking, "Hey, who's been hunting all the bears in the woods, and how can we stop this outrage?"

Yes, the answer to the bed question is Goldilocks. But until we can figure out why the bears are so perceptive with some things and clueless with others, that's all the answers they're getting from us.

———————— ◆ ————————

236. How many pickled peppers did Peter Piper pick?

None. The form of measurement in Peter's marketplace was indeed a peck. But, and this is interesting, he picked a peck of *pickled* peppers. The pickling process is something you do *after* you pick the peck of peppers.

It was impossible for poor Peter to pick a peck of pickled peppers as previously proposed precisely because Peter was by trade a piper and not a pepper pickler.

———————◆———————

237. Does anyone have the same Social Security number *and* nine-digit zip code?

Yes, but it's either a pure coincidence or the person moved to that zip code purposely in the hopes that the oddity might get him on David Letterman's show. Zip codes are assigned more or less geographically. They start at Agawam, Massachusetts, 01001xxxx and zigzag across the continent to Whale Pass, Alaska, at 99950xxxx. There are lots of gaps in the zip code roster to allow for future neighborhoods, towns, and cities, so there may not even be a zip code that matches your Social Security number.

———————◆———————

238. Why are manhole covers round?

So the cover doesn't fall into the hole. Let's say the hole is 36 inches in diameter and the cover that fits over it is 40 inches in diameter. No matter how you turn the cover, you can't get it to fit through the hole.

But if the hole is a 36-by-36-inch square and the cover is 40 inches square, the cover can fall in. If you slide the cover in diagonally, it'll disappear because the distance between diagonal corners of the hole is about 51 inches.*

◆

239. How does soap make things clean?

It doesn't dissolve the dirt. It doesn't scrub away the dirt. It works by making the dirt particles so slippery that they can't hold on to whatever you're cleaning.

◆

240. How do those little spokes on a bicycle wheel hold all that weight?

At any given moment, the spokes in the top half of the wheel hold the bike frame off the ground. (Actually, they hold up the hub, which holds on to the axle, which holds up the frame, but it's the same thing.) To test this theory, give your little brother a backpack loaded with bricks, then make him sit on the bike (tell him it's in the name of science). Then take a giant pair of metal shears and cut all the top spokes of the rear wheel at once.

Your next question should be, With all that weight hanging from those top spokes, why doesn't the wheel just collapse in half? Because the rim is round. To collapse, it would have to become an oval shape, which the spokes that happen to be on

---

*If you're a math whiz, you know that the diagonal forms the hypotenuse of two right triangles. Pick one of the triangles. To find the length of its hypotenuse, square the lengths of the two remaining sides. Add those two numbers. Then find the square root of that sum. The result is the length of the hypotenuse. In the example, the length of the hypotenuse is the square root of $36^2 + 36^2$, or about 51 inches.

the sides at that moment won't let it do. Skeptical? Dust off your little brother and put him on the handlebars (if you have a heavy-duty rim, stack a couple of his friends up there, too). Now cut the side spokes in the front wheel and see what happens.

What are the bottom spokes doing? Resting until it's their turn again. (Which is not a bad idea for your little brother: tomorrow we'll show you how hang gliders work.)

◆

241. What happens when you drive away with the gas nozzle still attached to your car?

You'd think that when the hose ran out of slack, it would yank the nozzle out of your car and flip it on the ground until someone came along and put it back in its holster on the side of the pump. You'd think.

Most likely, the angle of the nozzle in your car's filler pipe gives the car a better grip on the nozzle than the pump has on the hose. When you drive away, the hose is plucked from the pump, and a geyser of gasoline erupts in the gas station. It's easy to spot the idiot who caused the commotion—he's the one driving down the street with a gas nozzle hanging out of his car.

◆

242. If *October* means "eighth month," how come it's the tenth month of the year?

The Roman calendar originally considered March 1 as the first day of the year. Months seven through ten were given numerical names: September (7), October (8), November (9), and December (10). In 153 B.C. the elected officials began to take office on January 1, so they decided to consider that as the start of the year. But they kept the names the same.

◆

243. Why do some months have 30 days and others have 31?

In 46 B.C. Julius Caesar came up with a logical and easy-to-remember calendar. All the odd-numbered months had 31 days and all the even-numbered ones had 30, except February, which had 29. This added up to 365 days. (February got an extra day every fourth year to keep the calendar in line with the earth's rotation around the sun.)

But in 7 B.C. this beautiful system went to pieces. To honor the emperor Augustus, they named an entire month after him. They chose the month Sextilis because Augustus believed it was his lucky month.

Being the eighth month of the year, Sextilis had 30 days. But the month before it, July (named after his father-in-law, Julius), had 31 days. Not to be slighted, Augustus's month got 31 days, too—by stealing a day from February.

Of course, that created a whole new problem: three 31-day months in a row. To fix that, they took away September's 31st day and gave it to October, then took November's last day and gave it to December. What a mess!

We've been stuck with this silly system ever since. The first seven months of the year follow the 31-days-in-odd-months rule, but beginning with August, the even months get the extra day.

◆

244. How come Easter is celebrated sometimes in March and sometimes in April?

The date of Easter in a given year depends on both the solar and the lunar cycle. It takes place on the first Sunday following the first full moon after the spring equinox.

The equinox is easy to figure out; it's on March 21. But the moon follows its own 28-day cycle. If the moon happens to be full *on* the equinox, and the equinox falls on a Saturday, then Easter is on March 22—the earliest possible date for Easter. The latest it can occur is April 25.

If you're really crazy for math (especially algebra), here's how to determine the date of Easter in any given year. Begin by labeling the year *n*. Say the year you're curious about is 1994. So $n = 1994$. Now follow the instructions given in the column headings, reading one row at a time. In the first row, you are to *divide n by* 19. So first you divide 1994 by 19 (by hand—a calculator won't work for this part because you need a remainder). The result (or *quotient*) is 104. (You're not asked to label the quotient in this row, but in most rows you are.) The *remainder* (what's "left over" after dividing) is 18. You are to label the remainder *a*. So $a = 18$. Proceed in this manner row by row, labeling your results as indicated.

Divide	By	Label the Quotient	Label the Remainder
n	19		a
n	100	b	c
b	4	d	e
$b+8$	25	f	
$b-f+1$	3	g	
$(19 \times a)+b-d-g+15$	30		h
c	4	i	k
$32+(2 \times e)+(2 \times i)-h-k$	7		l
$a+(11 \times h)+(22 \times l)$	451	m	
$h+1-(7 \times m)+114$	31	p	q

The number of the month in which Easter falls is p; the day of the month is $q+1$. Wow.

245. What are the chances of being born on a leap day?

One in 1,461. In 1988, 9,792 babies were born on leap day. They'll celebrate their third "birthday" in the year 2000.

◆

246. How do magicians saw people in half?

There are two ways to do this trick. The first involves really sawing the person in half, which can only be done once.

The more common way is to use two assistants. While the first assistant climbs into the box from the stage, a second person climbs out of a trap in the bottom of the box and sticks her legs through the bottom of the box. Of course, the first assistant must fold her legs beneath her and conceal them in a trap in the top half of the box. Although the tables beneath the box look too thin to conceal a person, they're angled slightly to appear thinner than they are.

◆

247. What's the big deal about caviar?

Caviar is the salted eggs (roe) from fish in the sturgeon family. The biggest sturgeon is beluga. These fish average 800 pounds, and about 15 to 20 percent of that weight is roe. The fish are caught in nets and gutted. The roe is then removed and inspected, then packaged. Everything is done by hand, which adds to the price. The best caviar can go for $350 a pound. Not bad for salty fish eggs.

◆

248. How do they get lead in pencils?

A pencil looks like a solid piece of wood with a hole drilled through it for the lead. Actually, it's two pieces of wood. The lead is layed in a groove in the bottom half before the top half is glued on.

To make it even easier, pencil makers start with two rectangular slats of wood, a pencil's length long and several pencils' widths wide. Grooves are cut into each slat, the leads are layed, and the two halves are glued together. When the glue dries the slat is cut into individual pencils, which are milled to octagon or round shapes, painted, stamped with the company name, fit with erasers, and boxed for sale.

◆

249. How do movies get rated?

The Motion Picture Association of America established the rating system in 1968 to help parents figure out what movies would be appropriate for their kids. It's a voluntary thing— the government doesn't control the rating system, nor does it require it.

Here's how ratings are assigned: a board of film professionals views each film submitted for rating. These board members evaluate the movie on theme, language, nudity and sex, and violence.

◆

250. How do they pick the pope?

After waiting at least fifteen days after the death of the previous pope, all the big-time cardinals—over 100 men from around the world—gather in the Vatican in Rome to discuss who they think should be the pope. They stay locked in the

Vatican until they decide, partially to avoid the influence of powerful governments and special interest groups.

When it's time to vote, the cardinals fill out a secret ballot. The winner must receive a two-thirds majority plus one. If no one receives a majority, the balloting is repeated. If no one receives a majority this second time, the ballots are burned in a stove along with a chemical pellet that emits dark smoke. This signals to all the folks watching outside that no decision has been reached.

When a decision is finally reached, the ballots are burned in the stove again, this time with a chemical that emits white smoke. The world then knows that there's a new pope.

◆

251. How come little kids ask so many questions?

Because that's their job.

◆

252. What are the plastic things on six-packs called?

Even when begged, the Coca-Cola Company couldn't come up with a more interesting name than *carriers*. That's it. They're simply called carriers. It is amazing that something so simple in design and name can be so dangerous. When extracted from cans and carted away in whole form, those little plastic monsters become hangmen for animals that visit dump sites. So, cut up those carriers before they're carted.

◆

253. Why do you need to check the oil when the engine is warm?

Oil lubricates all the moving parts in the engine. When your car is turned off, the oil sneaks from the engine back to its home in the oil dish. When you check the oil level in a cold car an unusually high reading will occur, and you may need to add more oil than the dipstick indicates. The dipstick can't always be right—consider its name.

◆

254. Why aren't magazines arranged so that you can read an uninterrupted article?

It's a conspiracy. Magazine editors have banded together to annoy the general public. Okay, so there are some real reasons. Breaking the article can be used as a ploy to get you to look at the advertisements you might skip. Spacing is sometimes a problem, rendering it necessary to cause a skip. Color printing is expensive. It is sometimes cheaper to skip part of an article to a black-and-white page. Of course, I still believe that some editors receive perverse pleasure when they make you skip.

◆

255. Why does Ivory soap float?

Ivory soap—the slippery substance that gave you hours of pleasure when you carved it into toy boats and floated it in the tub—was an accident. According to Procter and Gamble legend, a worker left the soap-mixing machine on at lunchtime. When he returned, there was a frothy mess of goop in the tub. Instead of wasting the mixture, it was salvaged and sold. Consumers wrote to the company with grand excitement about the soap that floats. (It was 1879 and there was no TV.) So, Procter and Gamble kept up the whipping process that creates the soap that still affords us great pleasure.

◆

256. How does a polygraph machine work?

A polygraph machine measures a person's blood pressure, pulse, and respiration—all involuntary reactions. A pneumograph tube around the chest and a pulse cuff on the arm pick up impulses that are traced on moving graph paper.

The person being tested is asked questions relevant to the subject as well as simple questions where the answers will obviously be the truth. Sometimes the person is asked to lie so that the lie can be measured with other responses.

Whenever an involuntary response is abnormal after a reply, the response is assumed to be a lie. Of course, if you're being questioned in the manner, it's possible to assume that you're going to be nervous anyway, which is why many people do not believe in the validity of the test. You'd have to be a pretty cool cucumber to pass this exam.

◆

257. How do rock climbers stick to cliffs?

The wonders of modern technology have made it possible for climbers to do difficult and dangerous climbs. Early climbing gear was cumbersome and didn't help the process, but today, climbers wear specially-designed, smooth rubber-soled shoes that grip the rock. The more surface and weight placed on the rock, the more friction created for a strong foothold. Climbers step on the most improbable indentations and grasp the most minuscule ledges to propel themselves upward.

The most common type of climbing involves two climbers. The stronger climber is always the lead. The two wear harnesses and are attached by a springy nylon rope. The lead climbs and places metal pieces into cracks and crevices for protection. The metal pieces are attached to the rope with nylon runners and carabiners. The metal pieces come in different sizes and are carefully fitted into place. Some are so high tech that they have little springs that constrict and then contract to cling to the rock. The lead climber is safe as soon as she puts a piece of protection into the cliff face. Her partner may then belay her from the bottom in case she slips. The metal piece will prevent her from falling to the bottom, but she may still fall a good distance. Her partner can stop her from falling very far by one simple hand motion. He doubles his end of the rope through a metal piece known as a tuber or a figure eight, and he attaches the rope to his harness with a locking carabiner. He lets the rope out as the lead climbs, and he gives a tug if she happens to fall. This tug provides enough friction to make her stop.

---

258. What should you do if your car begins to overheat?

Your car can overheat for a plethora of reasons. It's a hot day. You're hot. The car's hot. Or you may have a pesky plumbing problem: a leaky hose, a blocked radiator, low water, or a bad thermostat valve. Before panic sets in, try a few simple things:

1. Turn the heater on. This draws heat away from the engine.
2. As soon as possible, turn in to a parking lot where you can get water. Your radiator evidently needs a drink.
3. Do not immediately take off the radiator cap unless you like burning hot geysers in your face.

4. Feel the rubber hosing that runs from the engine to the radiator. If the hosing is hard, there is too much pressure to remove the cap. If the hosing can be squished, it's safe to add water.

5. After adding water, your car should be happy. If the problem persists, drop two aspirin in the gas tank and call a mechanic in the morning.

———————— ◆ ————————

259. What does it take to rent an apartment?

It's a strange concept but true: Most landlords desire stable tenants on their property, and many believe that youth is a sign of instability. Your mission when apartment hunting is to convince the landlord that you will not corrupt the carpeting and then leave the country with no forwarding address. Here are some tips toward renting.

- Dress neatly. Leave the scorpion ring at home and put your green hair under a hat.
- Bring at least three references from stable people who can affirm your good character.
- If you haven't established credit, ask a parent or adult friend who does have credit to cosign the lease for you.

Before giving you the key to the apartment, a landlord may ask for:

- A security deposit equaling one half to one month's rent to be returned if you leave the property in good shape.
- The first month's rent up front.
- A lease stating your intent to stay for six months to a year, with thirty days advance notice to be given before you leave if you rent on a month-to-month basis.
- The last month's rent up front as well as the other money.

Renting is an expensive, as well as exciting, process. And once you rent that first place with great success, you'll be a less suspicious character in the landlord world.

NOTES

Body

1. Faculty of the UCLA School of Public Health.
2. *University of California, Berkeley Wellness Letter,* vol. 7, issue 11.
3. Faculty of the UCLA School of Public Health.
4. Ibid.
5. Dr. Kathleen Dillion.

College

1. *U.S. News & World Report,* February 27, 1989.
2. Ibid.
3. Ibid.

Death

1. Jerry Johnston, *Why Suicide?* (Nashville: Oliver-Nelson, 1987).

Divorce

1. Gary and Angela Hunt, *Mom and Dad Don't Live Together Anymore* (San Bernardino: Here's Life Publishers, 1989).
2. "Breaking the Divorce Cycle," *Newsweek,* January 13, 1992, pp. 48–53.

Family

1. Martha Farnsworth Riche, "Grown Children Return to Flexible Mothers," *Wall Street Journal,* March 29, 1991, p. B1.

Future

1. Alvin P. Sanoff with Joannie M. Schrof, "The Price of Victory," *U.S. News & World Report,* January 8, 1990, p. 52.
2. Database, *U.S. News & World Report,* December 31, 1990/ January 7, 1991, p. 12.

Learning

1. Gerald Coles, *The Learning Mystique* (New York: Ballantine, 1987).

Planet

1. Frances Moore Lappe, *Diet for a Small Planet* (New York: Ballantine, 1971).
2. Howard Gershe, "Sweet Charity," *Harper's Bazaar,* December 1991, p. 112.

Violence

1. Glenn Ruffenach, "At High Schools, One in Five Students Carries a Weapon," *The Wall Street Journal,* 11 October 1991, p. B5D. Article referred to a 1990 Centers for Disease Control Study, "Youth Risk Behavior Survey."

2. Kenneth D. Gadow and Joyce Sprafkin, "Field Experiments of Television Violence with Children," *Pediatrics,* Vol. 83, No. 3 (March 1989), p. 399.

3. Jim Hancock and Todd Temple, *Good Advice* (Grand Rapids, MI: Zondervan, 1987), p. 150.

Other Stuff

1. *UCB Wellness Letter,* vol. 7, issue 12.

— INDEX OF KEY WORDS —
(by question number)

THE AUTHOR

Todd Temple is the cofounder and executive director of 10 TO 20, a company that produces national events and conferences designed to get students involved in making a difference. He's written or cowritten nine books, including *Creative Dating* (a reasonably funny book celebrating the notion that there's more to dating than dinner and a movie) and *How to Become a Teenage Millionaire* (which actually is all about how to make, save, and spend money wisely). He's also a semi-regular contributor to teenage magazines and a motivational speaker to students at schools, churches, and conferences.

Todd holds a bachelor's degree in social ecology from the University of California, Irvine. His interests include literature, computers, theater, surfing, bicycling, travel, and hunger relief. He lives in Del Mar, California.